Simple Origami Airplanes

Fold 'em and Fly 'em

Andrew Dewar

TUTTLE PUBLISHING
Tokyo • Rutland, Vermont • Singapore

Contents

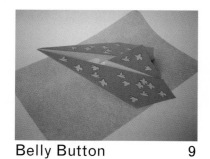

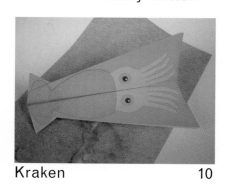

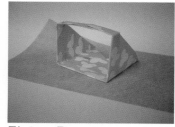

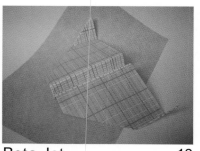

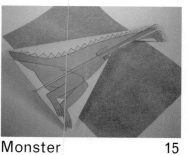

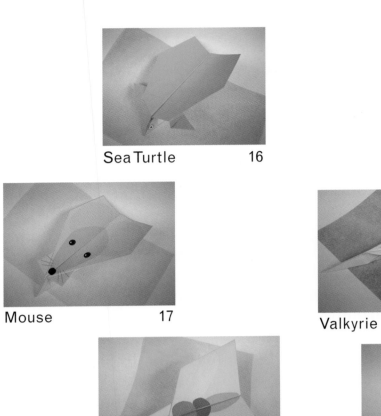

Sea Turtle   16

Interceptor   20

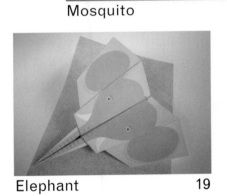

Mouse   17

Valkyrie   21

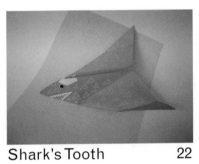

Mosquito   18

Shark's Tooth   22

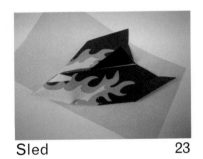

Elephant   19

Sled   23

Design Your Own Planes   24

Introduction

Isn't it amazing that an ordinary piece of paper can turn into an airplane? A real airplane, just like the ones that fly overhead every day?

Those airplanes, full of people flying here and there, have engines to help them take off and fly long distances. Paper airplanes may not have the engines, but if you fold them right and throw them carefully, they will fly just the same.

All airplanes need wings and balance. With origami planes, you get balance by folding your paper so that there are wings at the back, and lots of weight at the front.

This book is filled with directions for folding planes that will really fly, and paper you can use to make them. Even when the paper is gone and your airplanes have all flown away, you can use these directions with your own paper to make a whole new fleet of amazing origami airplanes.

How to Fold

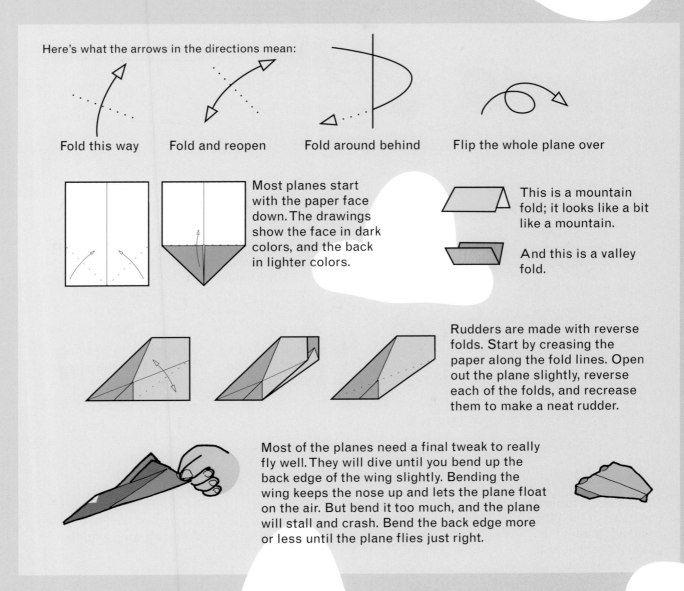

Here's what the arrows in the directions mean:

Fold this way   **Fold and reopen**   **Fold around behind**   **Flip the whole plane over**

Most planes start with the paper face down. The drawings show the face in dark colors, and the back in lighter colors.

This is a mountain fold; it looks like a bit like a mountain.

And this is a valley fold.

Rudders are made with reverse folds. Start by creasing the paper along the fold lines. Open out the plane slightly, reverse each of the folds, and recrease them to make a neat rudder.

Most of the planes need a final tweak to really fly well. They will dive until you bend up the back edge of the wing slightly. Bending the wing keeps the nose up and lets the plane float on the air. But bend it too much, and the plane will stall and crash. Bend the back edge more or less until the plane flies just right.

How to Fly the Planes

Your plane won't fly well unless it's straight. Hold it at arm's length and check.

If not, carefully twist the wings and tail until they are.

The plane will go from this...

...to this.

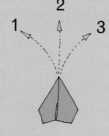

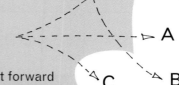

A

C   B

Test fly the plane by tossing it firmly straight forward and watching how it flies. If it stalls or dives, adjust it and test fly again, until it glides gently like line A.

A
Just right!

B
Fix a stall by bending the back of the wing down slightly.

C
Fix a dive by bending the back of the wing up slightly.

1   2   3

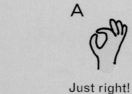

If your plane turns to one side or the other, adjust it until it flies straight as in line 2.

1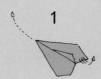
Fix a left turn by bending up the back edge of the right wing slightly.

2
Just right!

3
Fix a right turn by bending up the back edge of the left wing slightly.

Indoors, all you need is a gentle toss to get a good flight. Push the plane straight ahead, parallel to the floor, at about the speed you want your plane to travel.

If there is enough room, you can throw a little harder, but still basically straight ahead. Be sure not to hit anyone, break anything or poke any eyes!

On calm, dry days you can take your planes out to the park. Try throwing them straight up, as high as you can. This is how world record flights begin... except that they are made in sports stadiums. Can you beat 28 seconds?

Flying Wing

This is the simplest kind of airplane, just a wing. There are many real airplanes like it, such as the B-2 bomber. Pinch it between your fingers, push it forward, and see how far it can go!

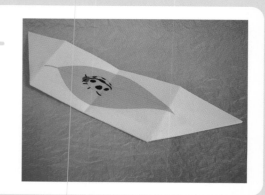

1
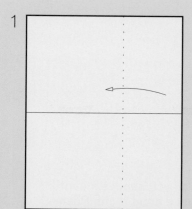
Start with the paper face down, and fold on line 1.

2
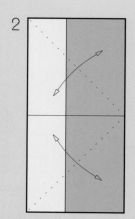
Fold on the 2 lines, and open the paper again.

3

Fold on the 3 lines.

4
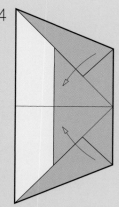
Refold on the 2 lines.

5
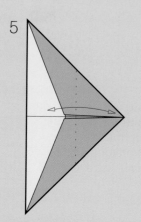
Fold on line 4, and open the paper again.

6
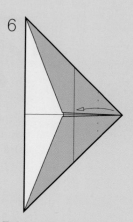
Fold on line 5.

7
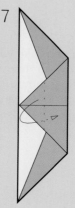
Tuck the triangle inside all the other layers of paper.

8
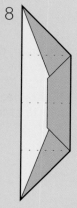
Fold lightly on the 6 lines, and make a slight mountain fold at the center.

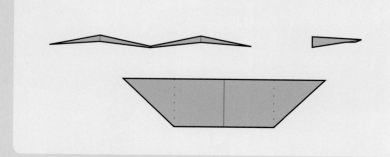

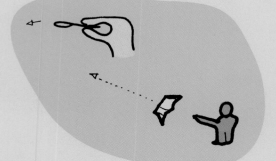

Belly Button

In the West, the best-known paper airplane is the dart. In Japan, where origami started, it's the navel airplane. The triangle at the bottom is the belly button, which holds everything together. This is an improved version of the classic.

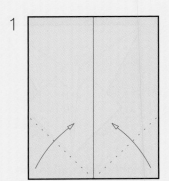

1 Start with the paper face down, and fold on the 1 lines.

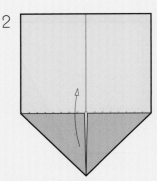

2 Fold up at the 2 line.

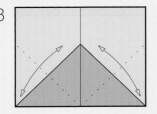

3 Fold on the 3 lines, and open the paper again.

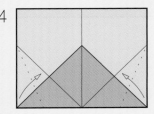

4 Fold on the 4 lines.

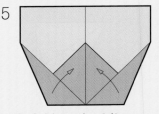

5 Refold on the 3 lines.

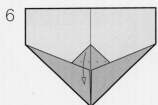

6 Fold down the belly button on line 5.

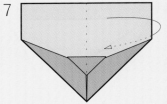

7 Mountain fold the plane along the centerline.

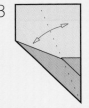

8 Fold down the wing at line 6, and open the paper again.

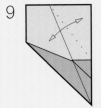

9 Fold the rudder on line 7, and open the paper.

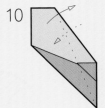

10 Reverse fold the rudder and refold the wings.

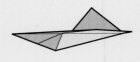

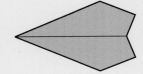

Kraken

The kraken is a giant squid that lives in the ocean depths; the Kraken is a sleek airplane that lives in the open sky. It's based on another Japanese classic: the squid plane, which looks a bit a squid jetting through the water.

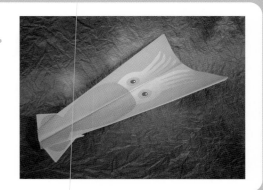

1
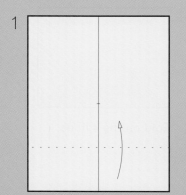
Start with the paper face down, and fold on line 1.

2

Fold on the right 2 line.

3
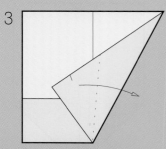
Fold on the right 4 line. Line 3 will meet the edge.

4
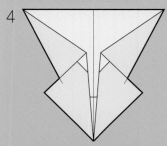
Fold the left half in the same way.

5
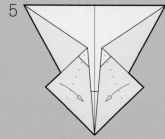
Fold on line 5.

6
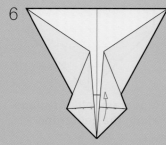
Fold on line 6.

7
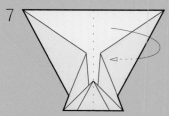
Mountain fold along the centerline.

8
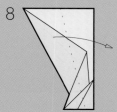
Fold the wings at the 7 lines.

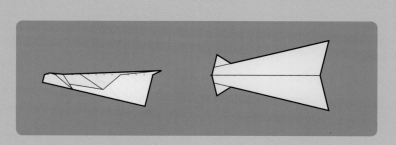

Flying Box

Almost anything will fly, if it has wings and the balance is right. Will this box fly too? Fold it and see for yourself!

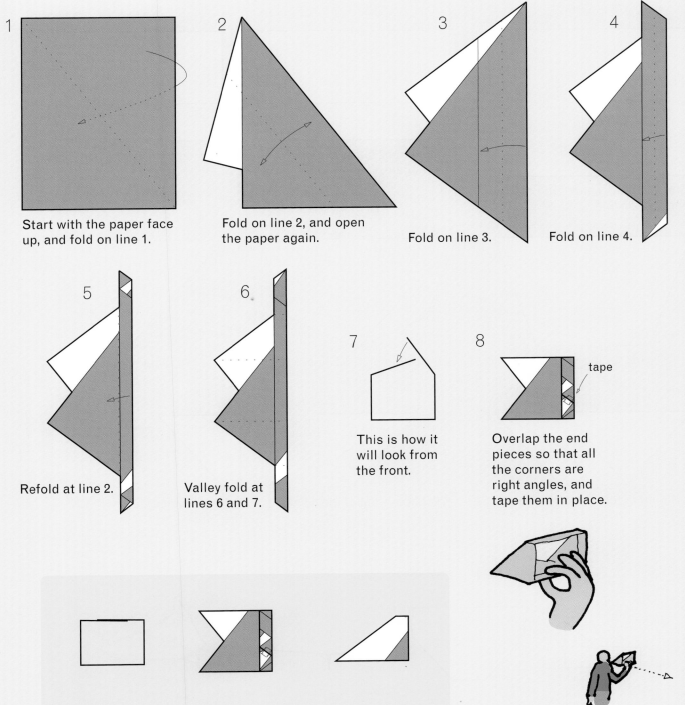

1 Start with the paper face up, and fold on line 1.

2 Fold on line 2, and open the paper again.

3 Fold on line 3.

4 Fold on line 4.

5 Refold at line 2.

6 Valley fold at lines 6 and 7.

7 This is how it will look from the front.

8 Overlap the end pieces so that all the corners are right angles, and tape them in place.

tape

Beta Jet

A big wing and two pointy rudders: this plane looks fast. Take it outside and throw it hard and high. It will really soar. Try folding the rudders down instead of up, and see which flies better!

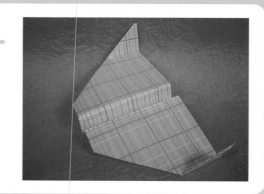

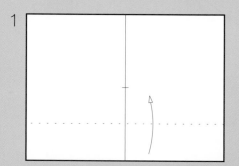

1

Start with the paper face down, and fold on line 1.

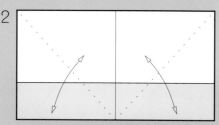

2

Fold on the 2 lines, and open the paper again.

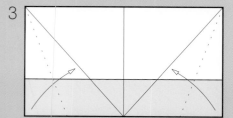

3

Fold on the 3 lines.

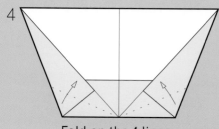

4

Fold on the 4 lines.

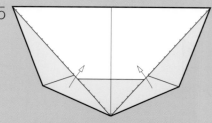

5

Refold on the 2 lines.

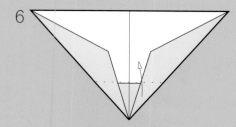

6

Fold on line 5.

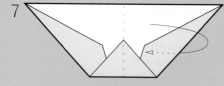

7

Mountain fold the centerline.

8

Fold the wing at the 6 lines.

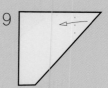

9

Fold the rudders at the 7 lines.

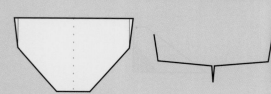

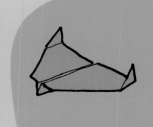

Star Shuttle

When airplanes start flying to space and back, they may well look like this. The rudders point down for stability, and the wings are swept back for speed. But this shuttle will float across your living room.

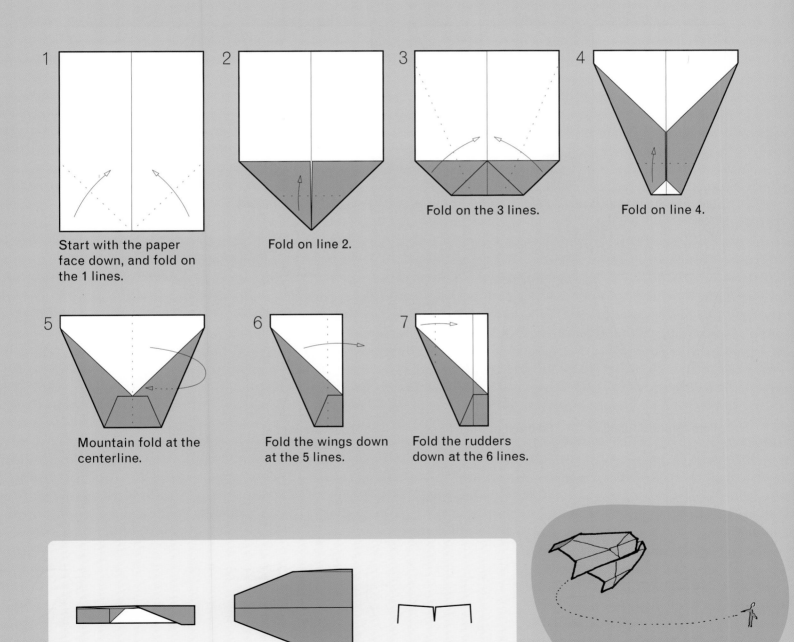

1 Start with the paper face down, and fold on the 1 lines.

2 Fold on line 2.

3 Fold on the 3 lines.

4 Fold on line 4.

5 Mountain fold at the centerline.

6 Fold the wings down at the 5 lines.

7 Fold the rudders down at the 6 lines.

Sea Serpent

This plane looks strange, but it is surprisingly easy to fly. It is basically a squid with wings folded in to give it a long neck. Every few flights you should repeat step 8 to keep the wings straight.

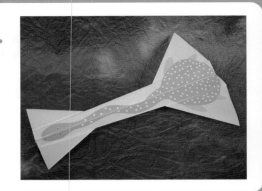

1
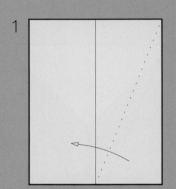
Start with the paper face down, and fold on the right line 1.

2
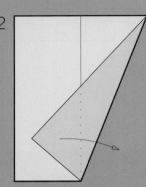
Fold on the right line 2.

3
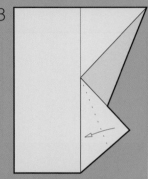
Fold on the right line 3.

4
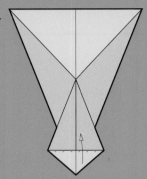
Fold the left side the same way. Fold on line 4.

5
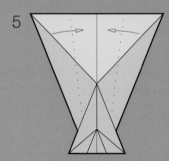
Fold on the 5 lines.

6
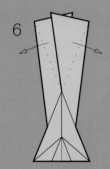
Fold out at the 6 lines.

7
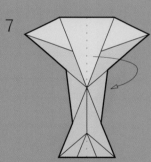
Mountain fold at the centerline.

8
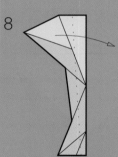
Fold the wings out at line 7.

 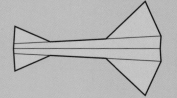 

Monster

Here there be monsters! When you take this plane to the park, everyone will wonder how it can fly. But as long as the left side balances the right, a plane can be any shape you like—even half dart and half squid.

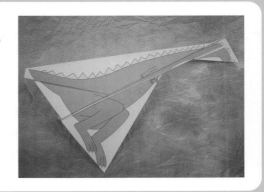

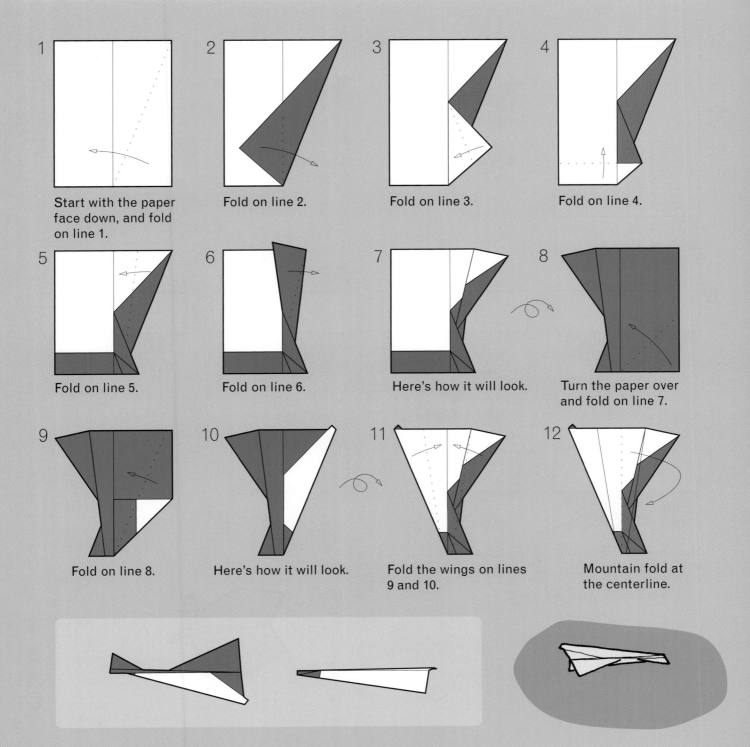

1 Start with the paper face down, and fold on line 1.

2 Fold on line 2.

3 Fold on line 3.

4 Fold on line 4.

5 Fold on line 5.

6 Fold on line 6.

7 Here's how it will look.

8 Turn the paper over and fold on line 7.

9 Fold on line 8.

10 Here's how it will look.

11 Fold the wings on lines 9 and 10.

12 Mountain fold at the centerline.

Sea Turtle

Water is a fluid very much like air, and many animals fly through water just as birds and bats fly through the air. Sea turtles use their flippers like wings, and flap gracefully through the sea. This plane doesn't flap, but it sure does fly!

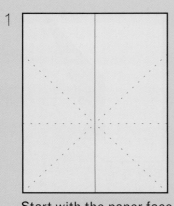
1

Start with the paper face down, and fold on lines 1, 2, and 3.

2

Repeat the folds like this.

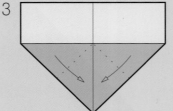
3

Fold down the corners on the 4 lines.

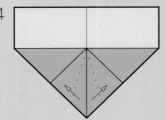
4

Fold the corners back out on the 5 lines.

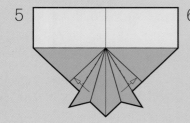
5

Fold on the 6 lines.

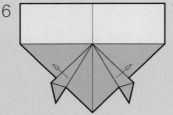
6

Refold at the 4 lines.

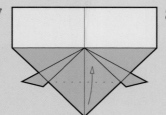
7

Fold up at line 7.

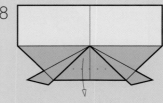
8

Fold down at line 7.

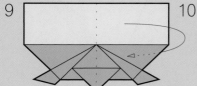
9

Mountain fold the plane at the centerline.

10

Fold the wings at the 9 lines.

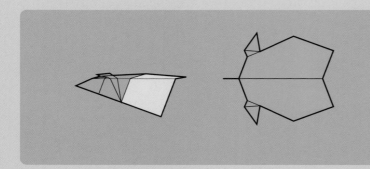

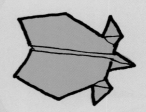

Mouse

This plane is very simple and flies well, but it looks unusual, like the face of a mouse, or maybe a fox. You need to recrease the wing folds every few flights.

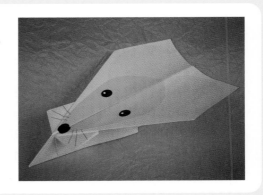

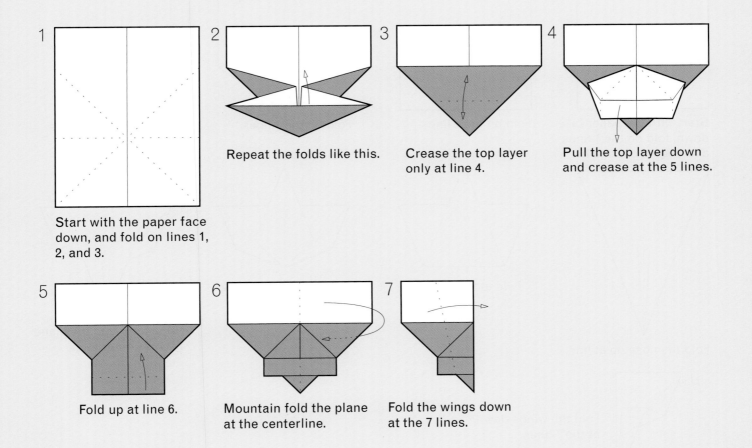

1

Start with the paper face down, and fold on lines 1, 2, and 3.

2

Repeat the folds like this.

3

Crease the top layer only at line 4.

4

Pull the top layer down and crease at the 5 lines.

5

Fold up at line 6.

6

Mountain fold the plane at the centerline.

7

Fold the wings down at the 7 lines.

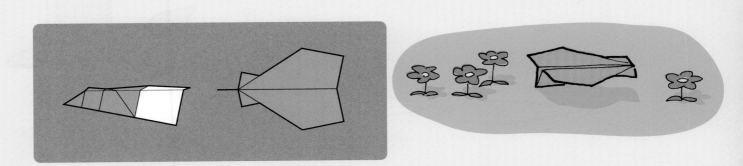

Mosquito

Real mosquitos are not very good at flying; they are slow and don't like wind. But this plane has lots of weight in the nose, so it flies fast and straight, indoors or out. Be sure not to hit anyone with that sharp nose!

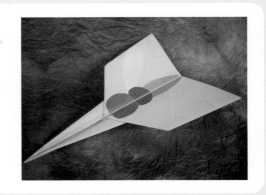

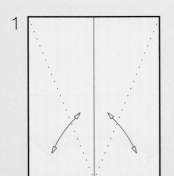

1 Start with the paper face down, fold on the 1 lines, and open it out again.

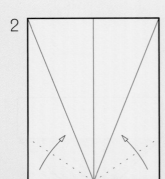

2 Fold on the 2 lines.

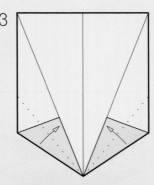

3 Fold on the 3 lines.

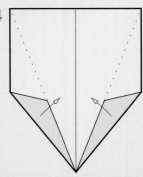

4 Refold on the 1 lines.

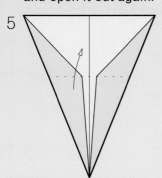

5 Fold the nose up at line 4.

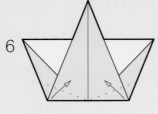

6 Fold at the 5 lines.

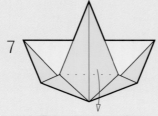

7 Fold the nose back down at line 6.

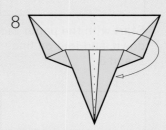

8 Mountain fold the plane at the centerline.

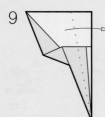

9 Fold the wings down at the 7 lines.

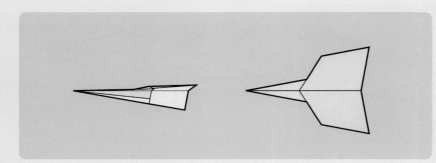

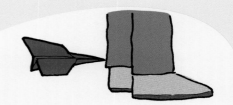

Elephant

A long trunk, a big face, and wide, floppy ears. No doubt about it, this is an elephant! The ears give it extra lift, so it floats gently across the room. It is best to fly this one indoors.

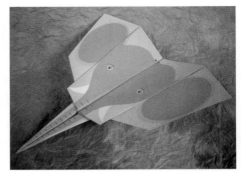

1

Start with the paper face down, and fold on the 1 lines.

2

Fold on the 2 lines.

3

Fold on the 3, and open the paper out again.

4

Fold the ears down at the 4 lines.

5

Refold line 3.

6

Fold the nose down at line 5.

7

Mountain fold at the centerline.

8

Fold the wings down at the 6 lines.

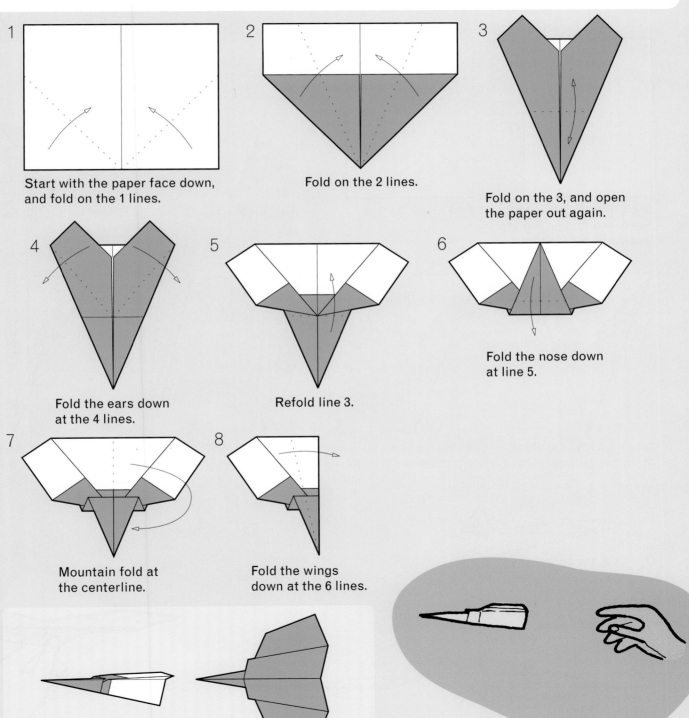

Interceptor

This sleek plane looks like a jet fighter. You can throw it hard outdoors, or fly it gently indoors. It will fly even faster and look more realistic if you tape the back of the rudder together.

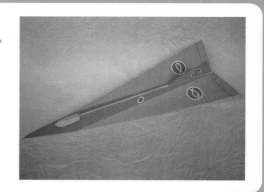

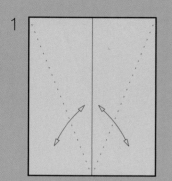

1 Start with the paper face down, and fold on the 1 lines, and open it again.

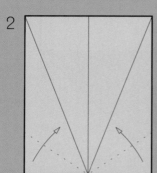

2 Fold on the 2 lines.

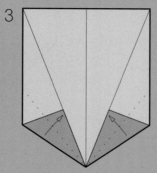

3 Fold on the 3 lines.

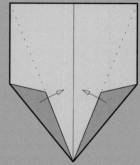

4 Refold on the 1 lines.

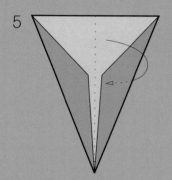

5 Mountain fold the plane at the centerline.

6 Fold the top layer down at line 4.

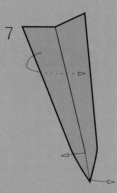

7 Bend the nose to reverse the direction of the fold, and fold the other line 4.

8 Fold the wings up at the 5 lines.

9 Fold the rudder up at line 6, and reverse fold it.

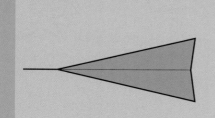

10 Open out the wings.

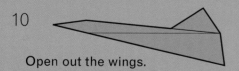

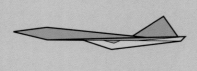

Valkyrie

The delta wing and twin rudders on this plane remind me of the XB-70 Valkyrie, an experimental bomber that could fly three times the speed of sound. This Valkyrie is fast too, and flies best outdoors with a strong throw.

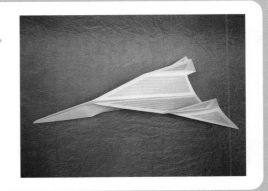

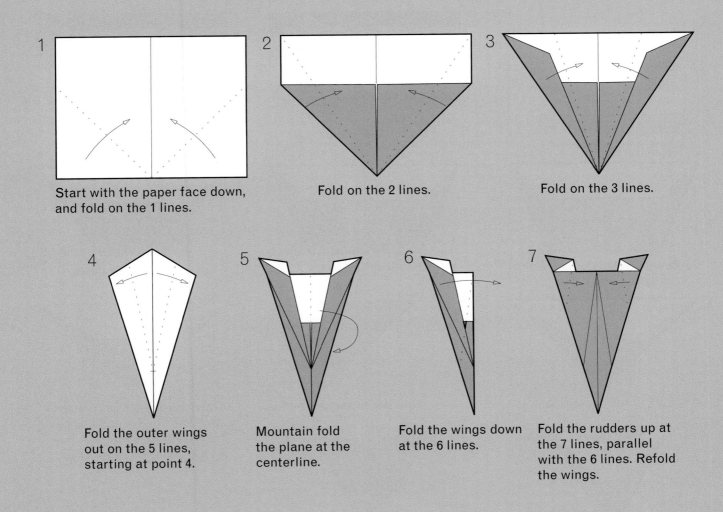

1

Start with the paper face down, and fold on the 1 lines.

2

Fold on the 2 lines.

3

Fold on the 3 lines.

4

Fold the outer wings out on the 5 lines, starting at point 4.

5

Mountain fold the plane at the centerline.

6

Fold the wings down at the 6 lines.

7

Fold the rudders up at the 7 lines, parallel with the 6 lines. Refold the wings.

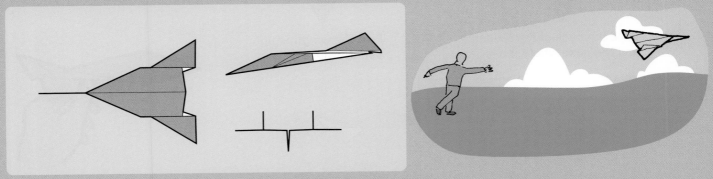

Shark's Tooth

With a little tape, you can turn a dart into a plane with a three-dimensional fuselage, like a stealth jet or a space shuttle. This plane looks wild and ferocious, but it is really quite steady and gentle, indoors or out.

1

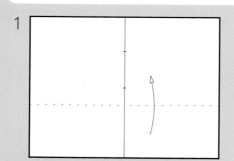

Start with the paper face down, and fold on line 1.

2

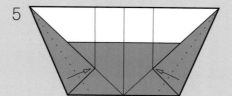

Fold on the 2 lines, and open the paper out again.

3

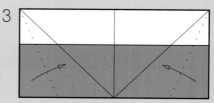

Fold on the 3 lines.

4

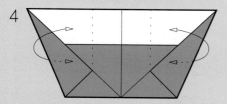

Mountain fold on the 4 lines, and open them again.

5

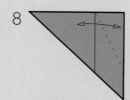

Fold on the 5 lines.

6

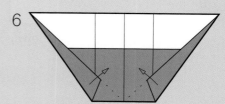

Refold on the 2 lines.

7

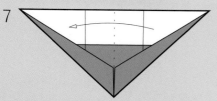

Fold at the centerline.

8

Fold the rudder at line 6.

9

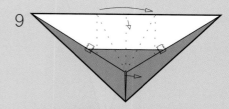

Open out the plane, tape the wings as shown, and pull the back edge together with the rudder pointing towards you.

10

tape

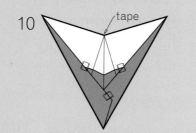

Tape the back of the rudder, and the nose where it overlaps.

11

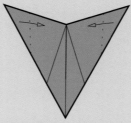

Fold the wingtips up slightly at the 7 lines.

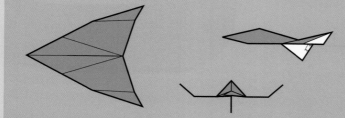

Sled

Don't these upturned wingtips remind you of a sled? But this plane also looks like it could slide down from space to a nice soft landing. How high can you make it go?

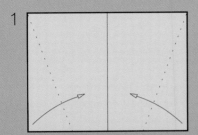

1 Start with the paper face down, and fold on the 1 lines.

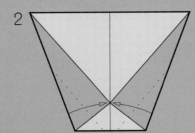

2 Fold on the 2 lines.

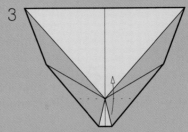

3 Fold on line 3.

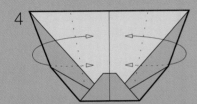

4 Mountain fold on the 4 lines, and open them again.

5 Fold the plane together at the centerline.

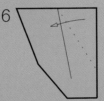

6 Fold the rudder at line 5.

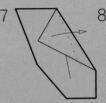

7 Fold it again at line 6.

8 Here's how it will look.

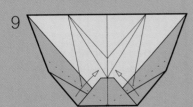

9 Open out the plane, and fold on the 7 lines.

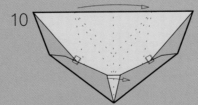

10 Tape the wings as shown and pull the back edge together. The rudder should be double reverse folded.

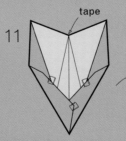

tape

11 Tape the back of the rudder, and the nose where it overlaps.

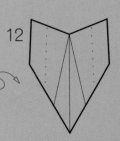

12 Fold up the wingtips at the 8 lines.

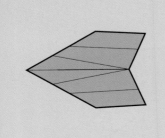

Design Your Own Planes

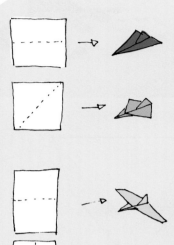

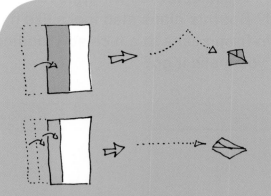

The kind of paper you use and the direction of the center fold will determine the shape of your plane. Square paper makes compact planes: triangular planes from straight folds, and diamonds from diagonal folds. Rectangular paper lets you make short and wide or long and pointy planes.

Balance is very important. The front of your plane needs to be heavy, which means folding lots of layers of paper. If your plane stalls, make extra folds at the front to improve the balance.

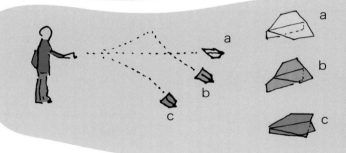

Your plane might not fly right away, but don't give up yet! You can refold the wings to change the balance and add stability. Plane "a" is just right. You can fix planes that stall (like "b") by making the wings a little smaller at the front or bigger at the back. Planes that dive (like "c") can be fixed by making the back part of the fuselage bigger and changing the balance.

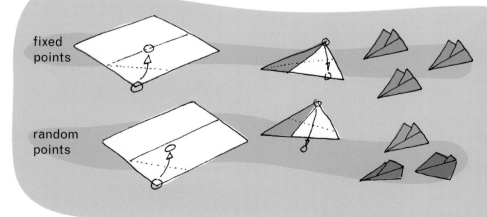

fixed points

random points

Once your plane starts really flying, you'll want to make more. But if you've just folded randomly, your next plane won't be quite the same. Always fold to fixed points—edge to edge, corner to corner, corner to edge, or at half-way points —and every plane will turn out just right.

If your planes still don't fly, just wad them up and toss them... You can always start again with a fresh sheet of paper.

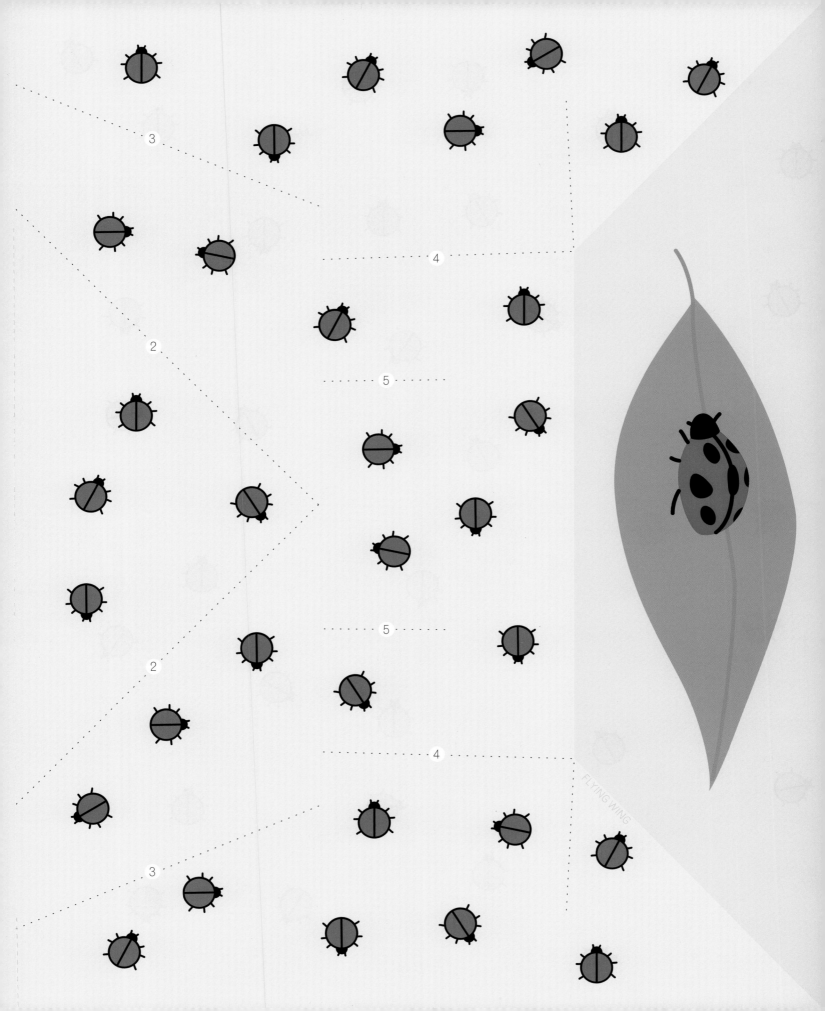

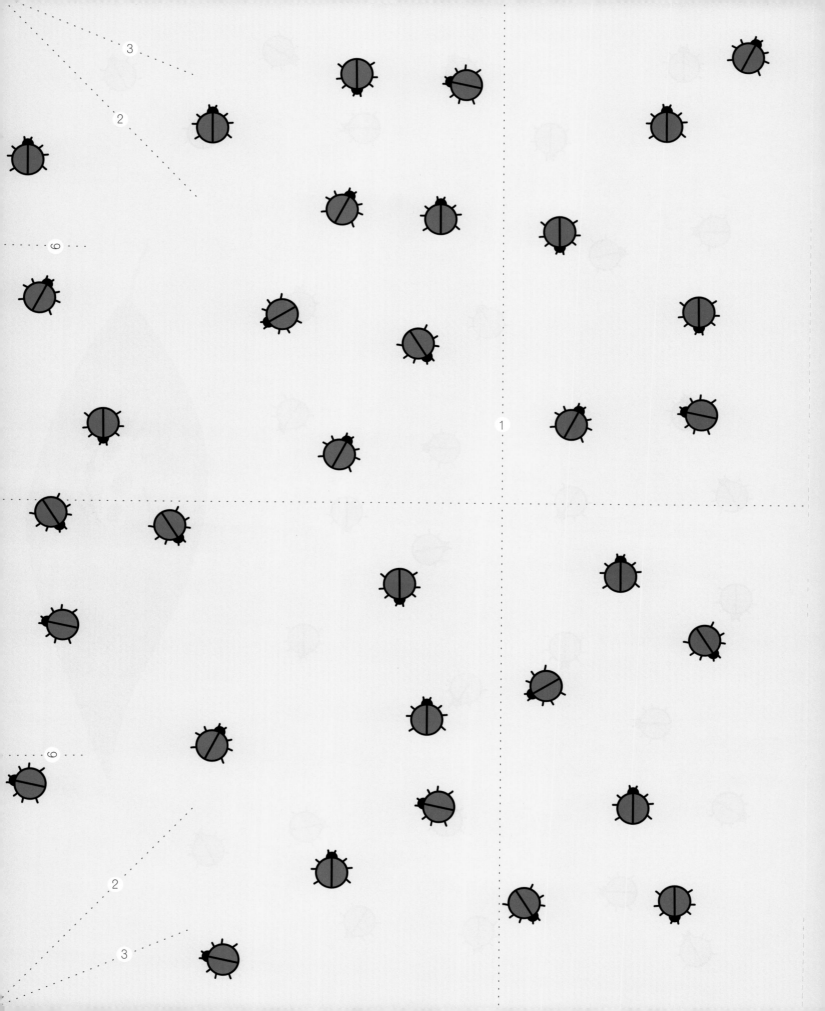

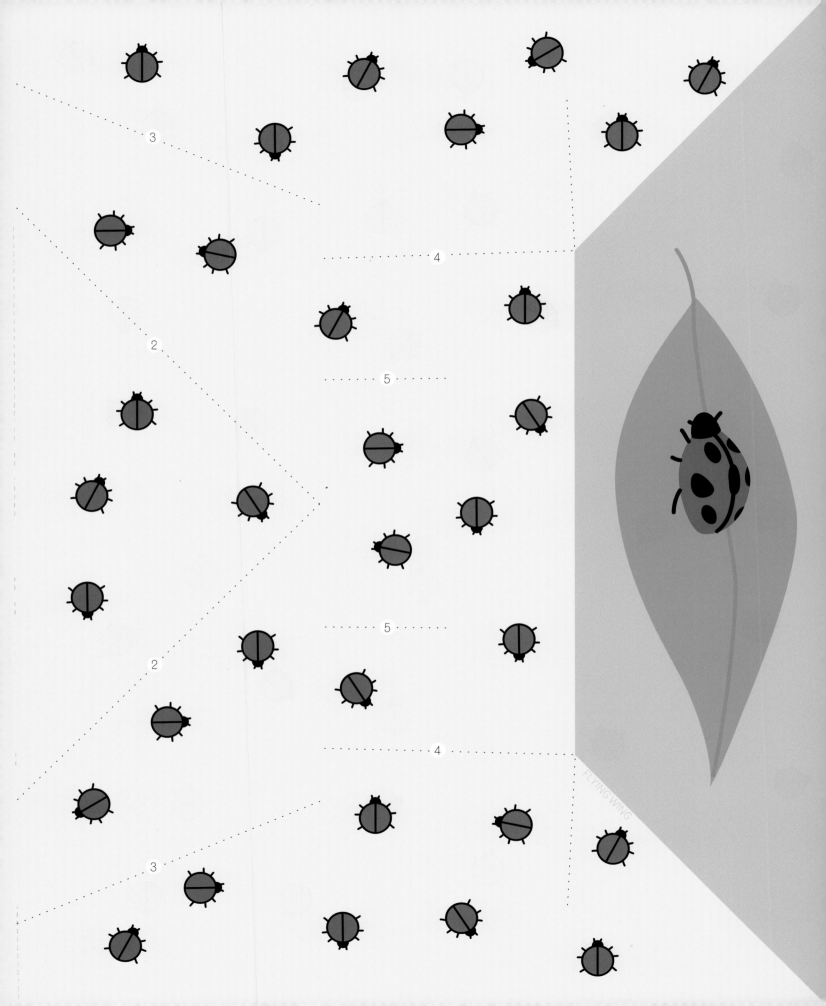

FLYING WING

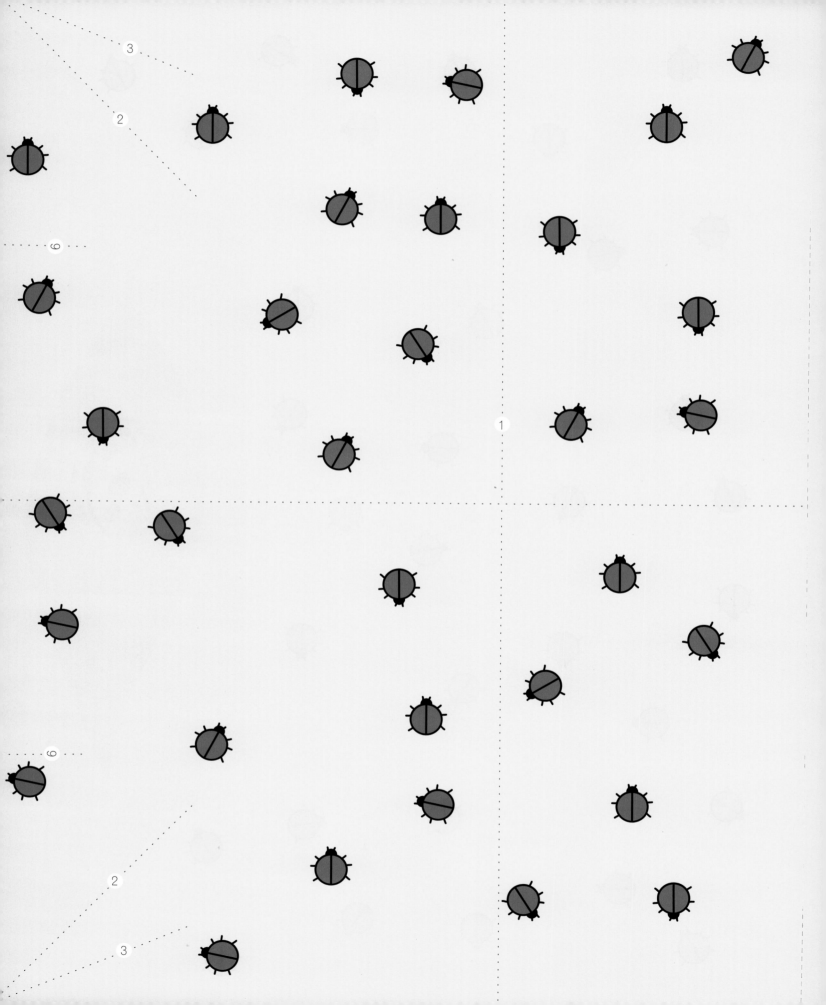

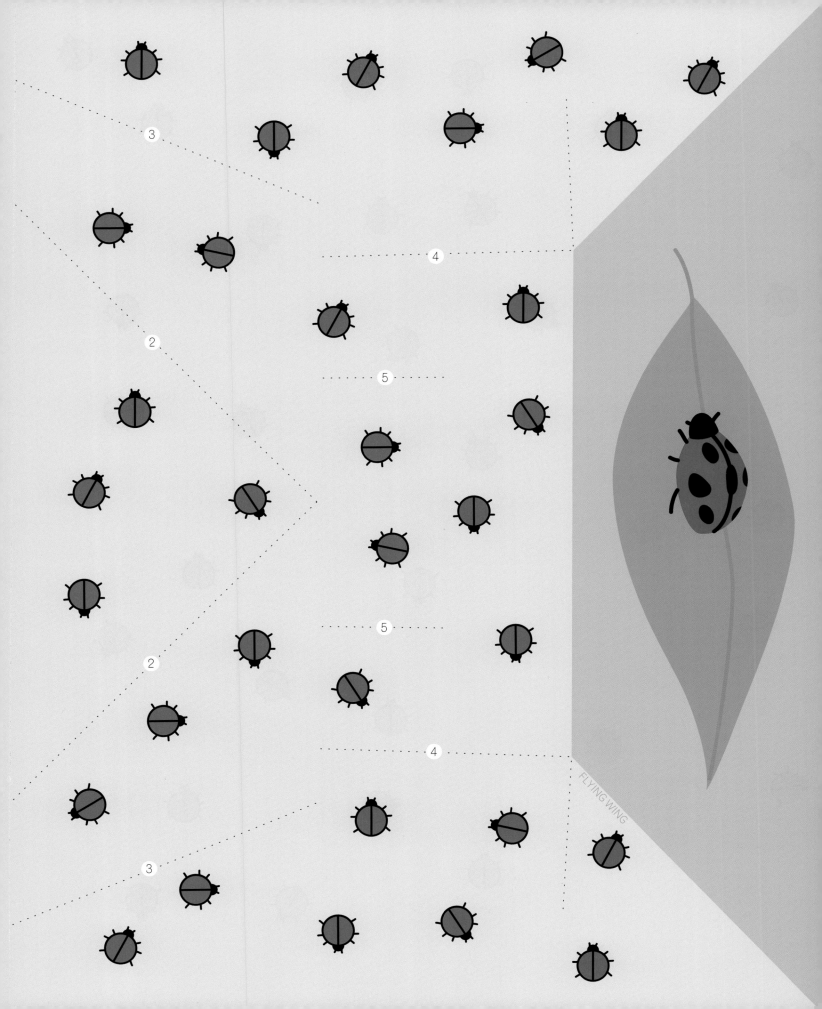

FLYING WING

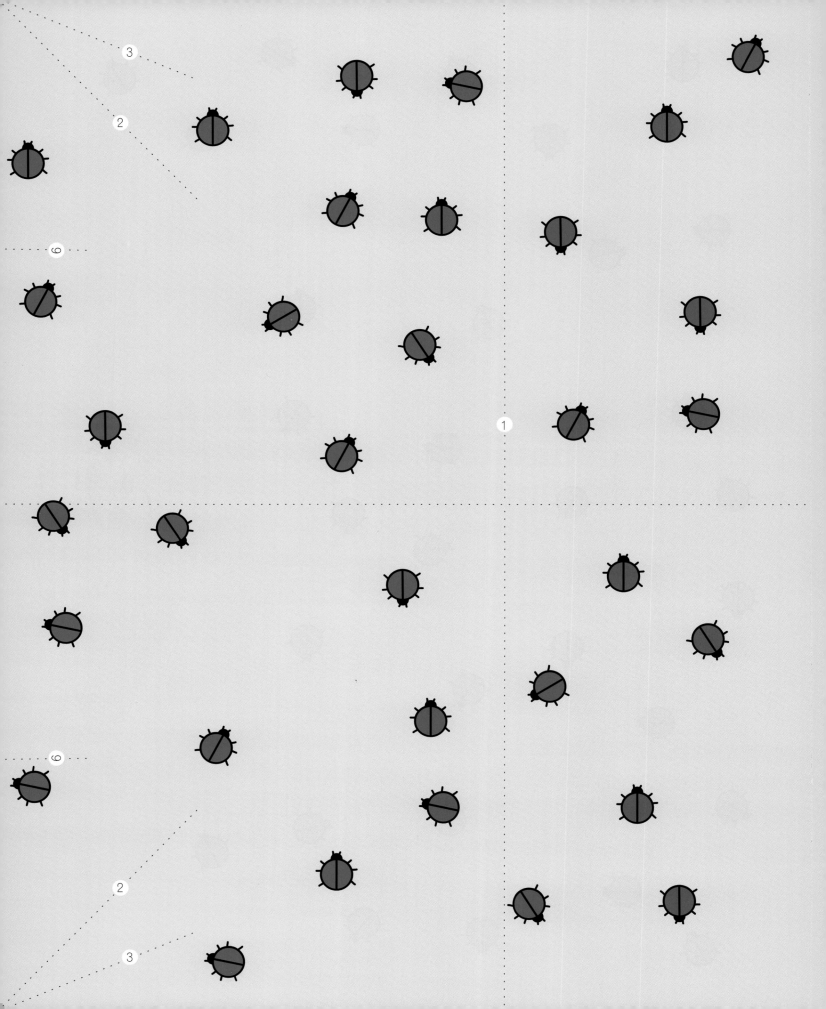

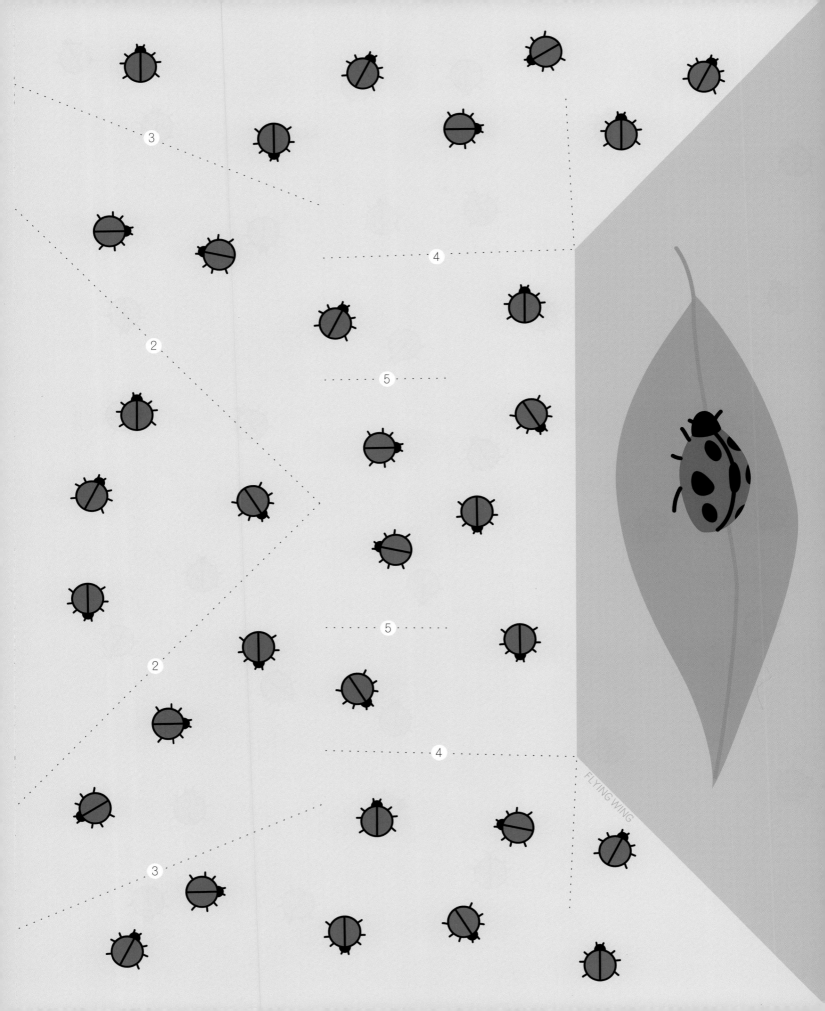

FLYING WING

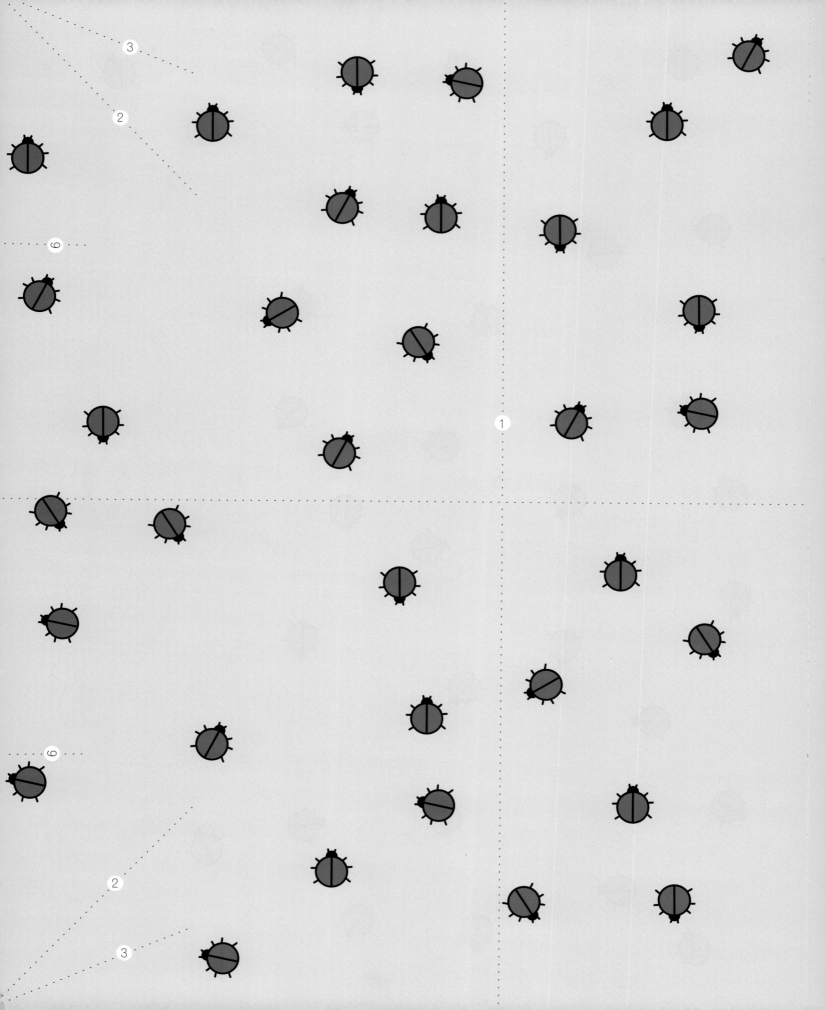

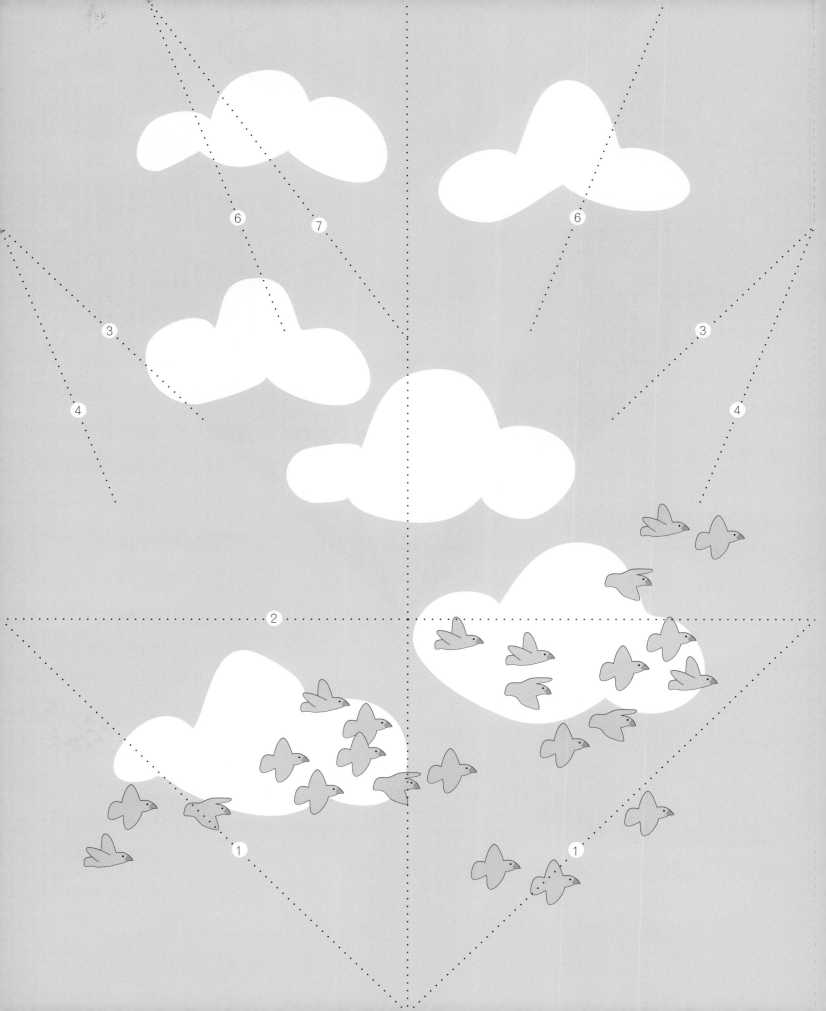

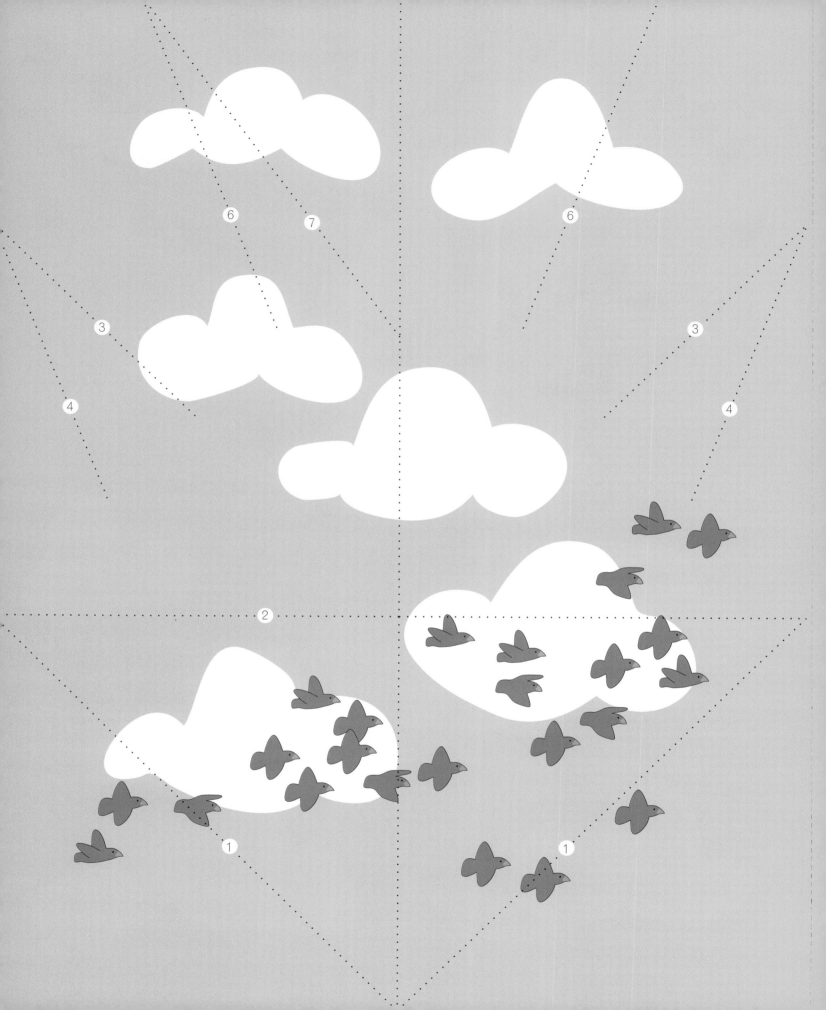

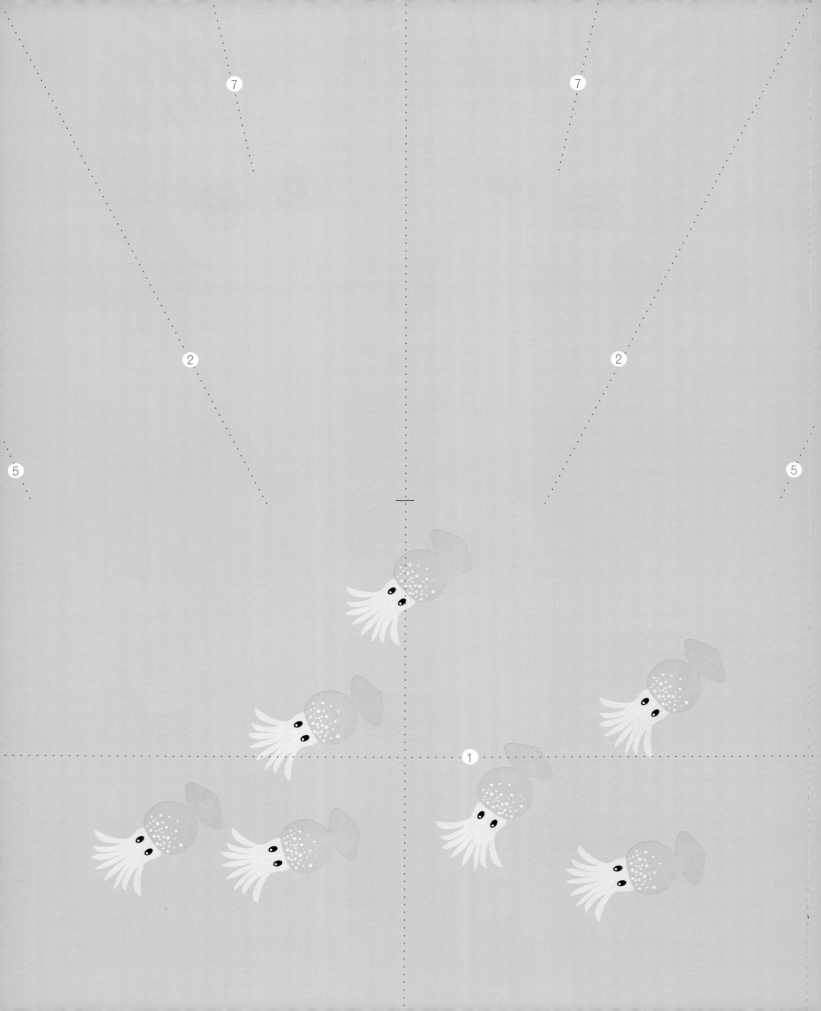

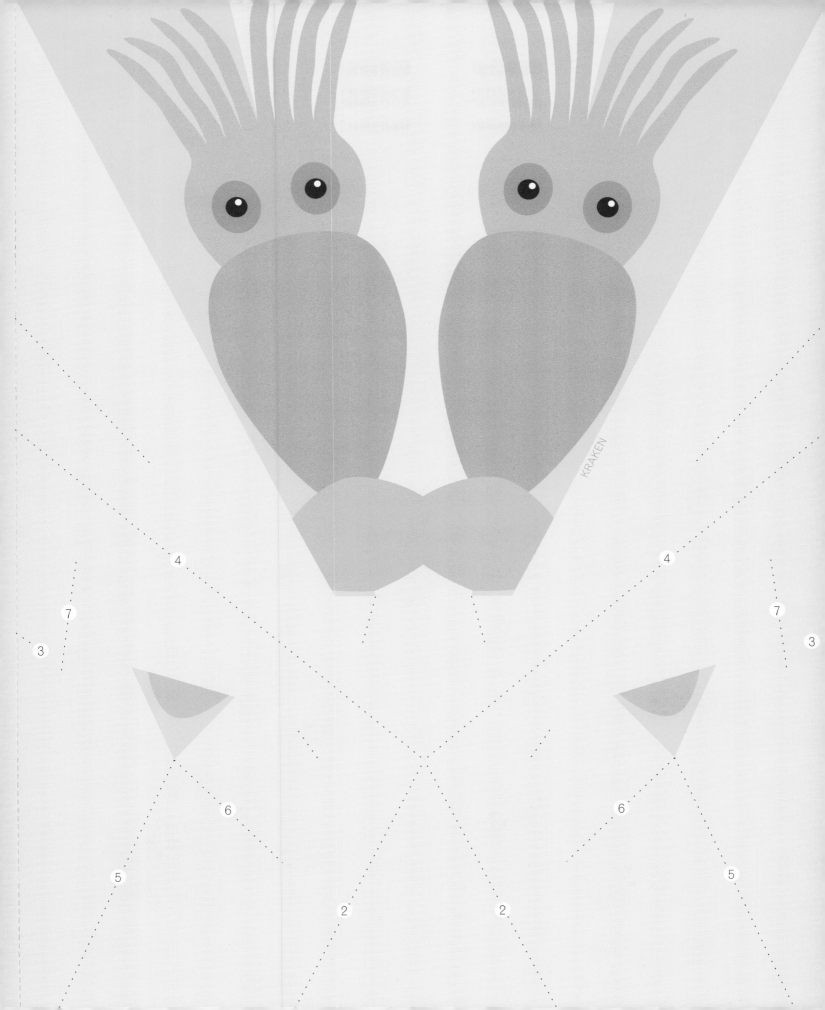

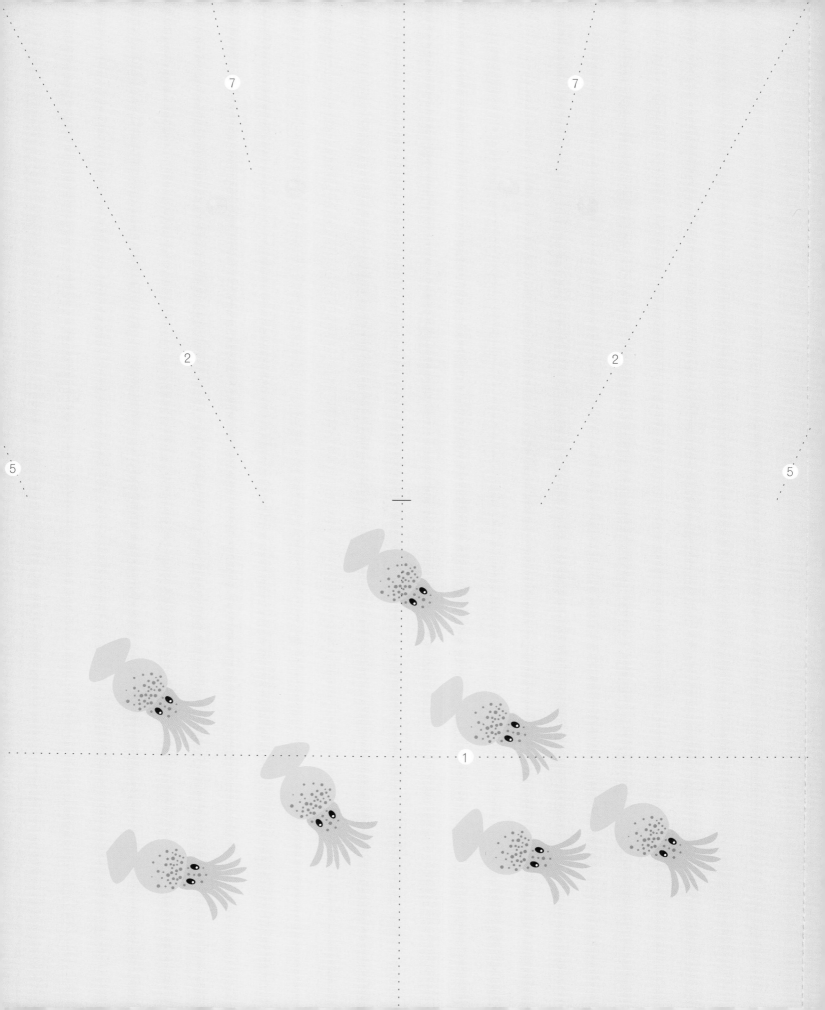

FLYING BOX

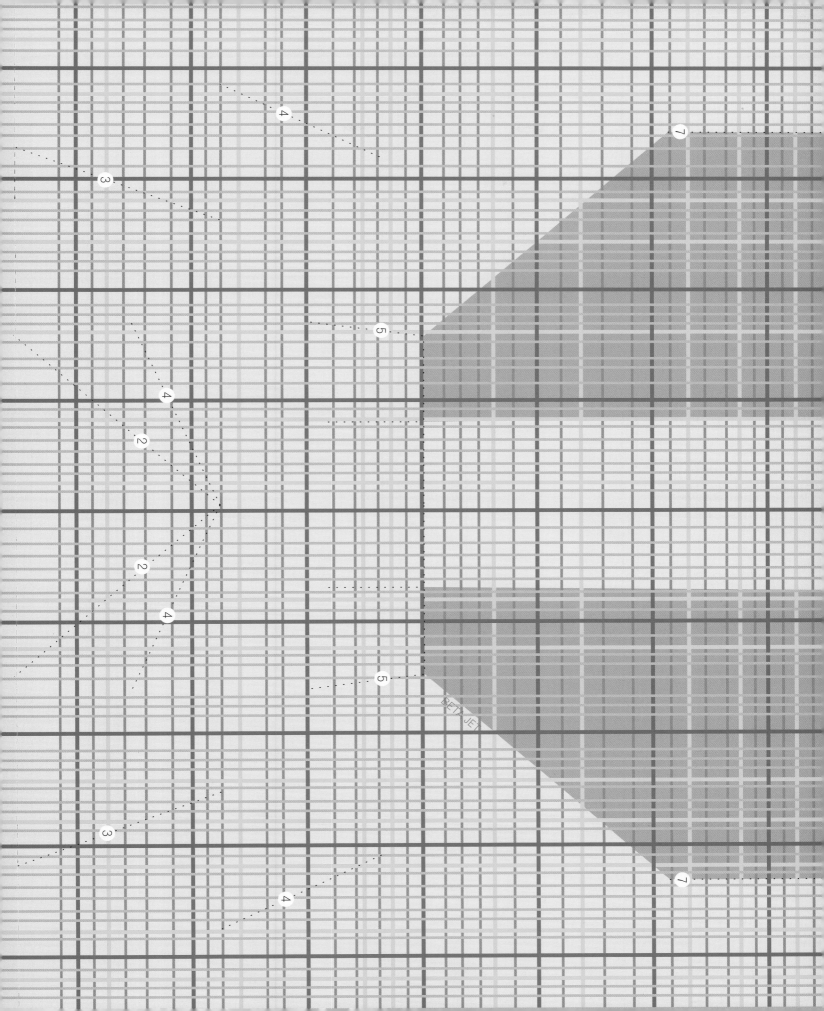

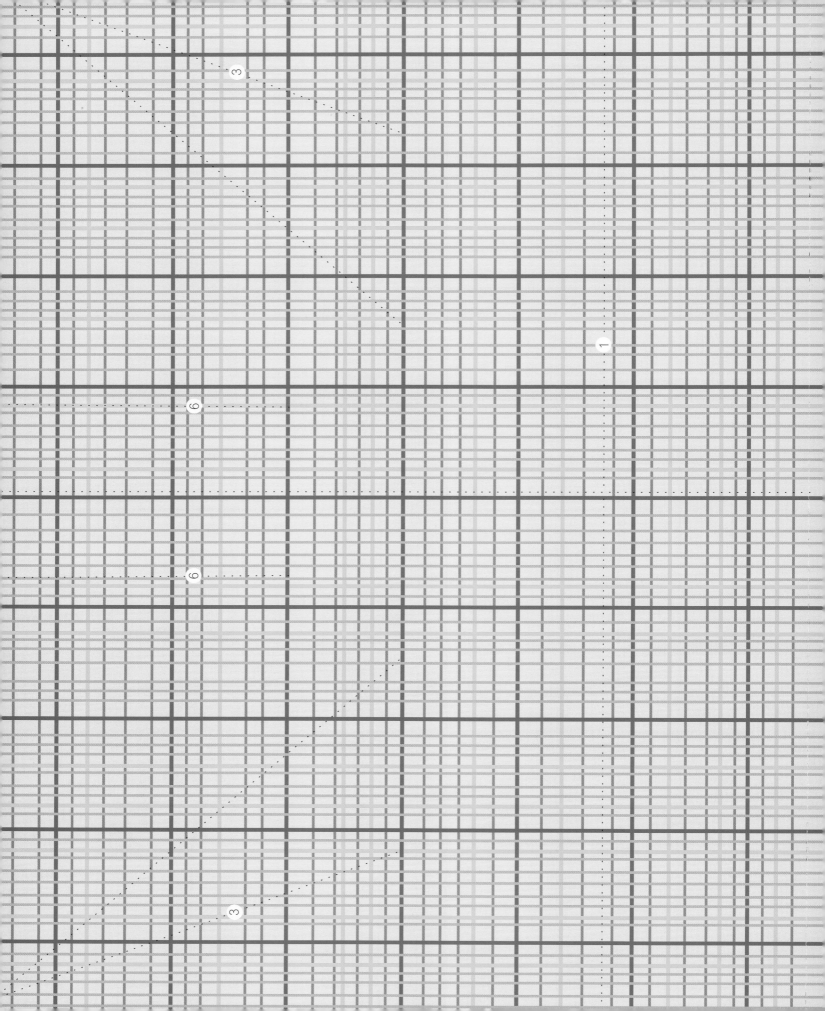

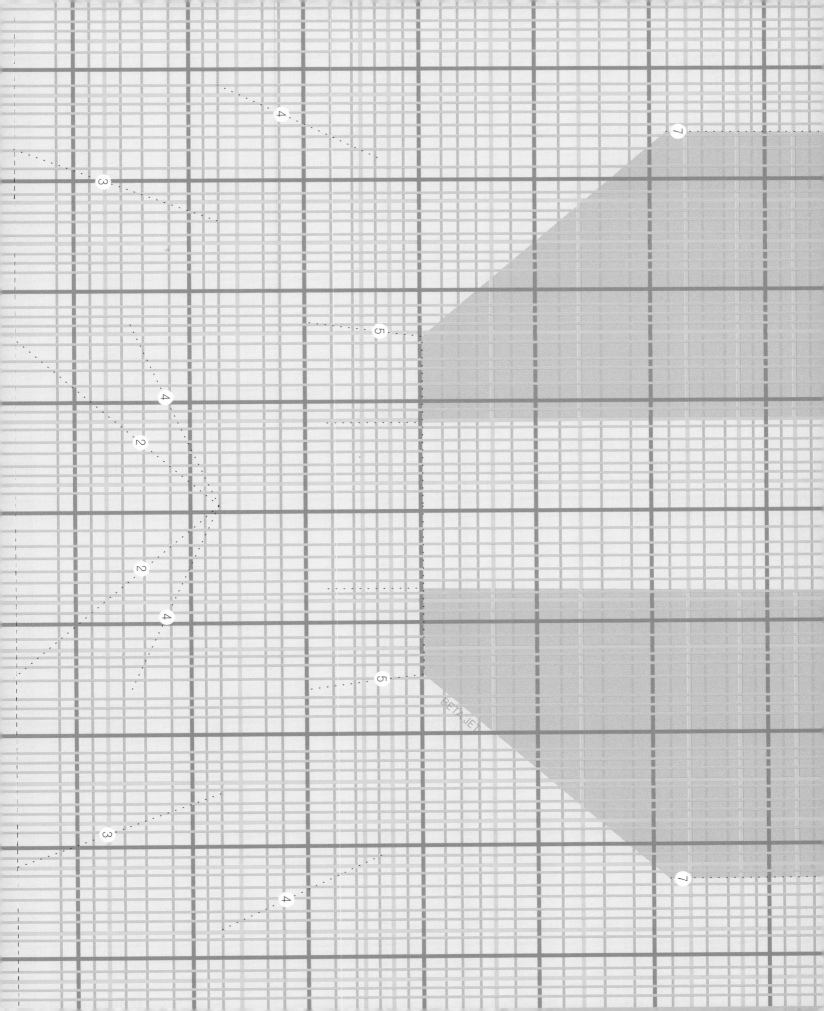

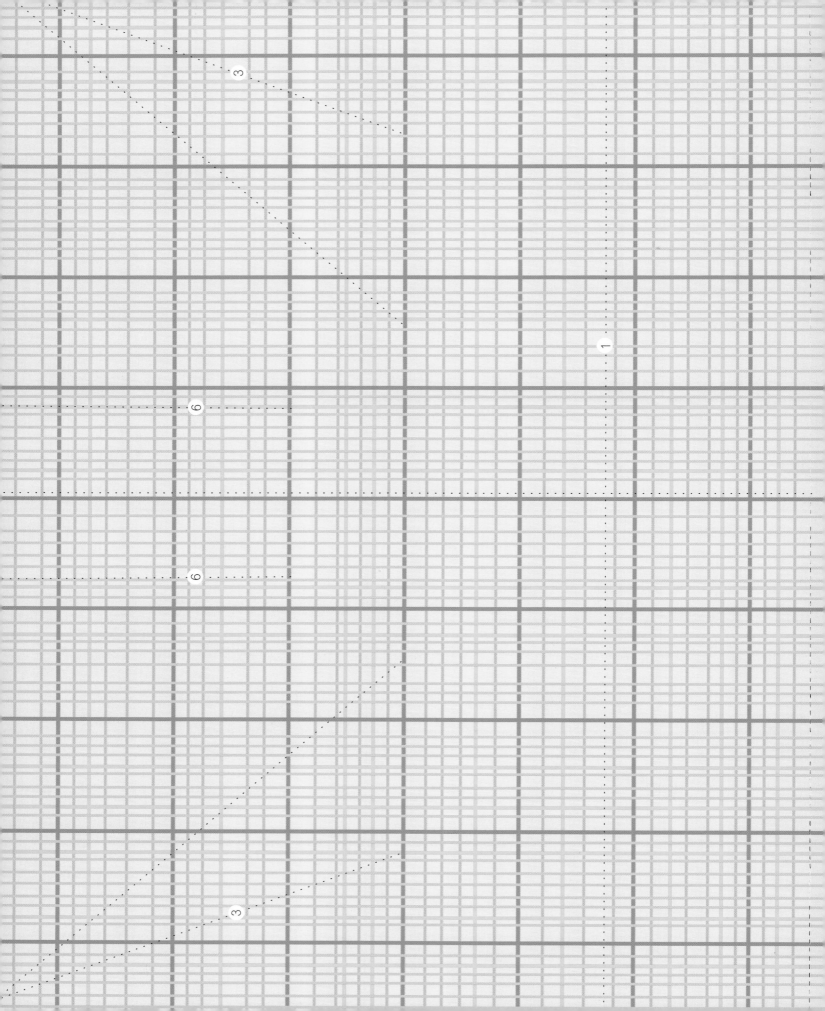

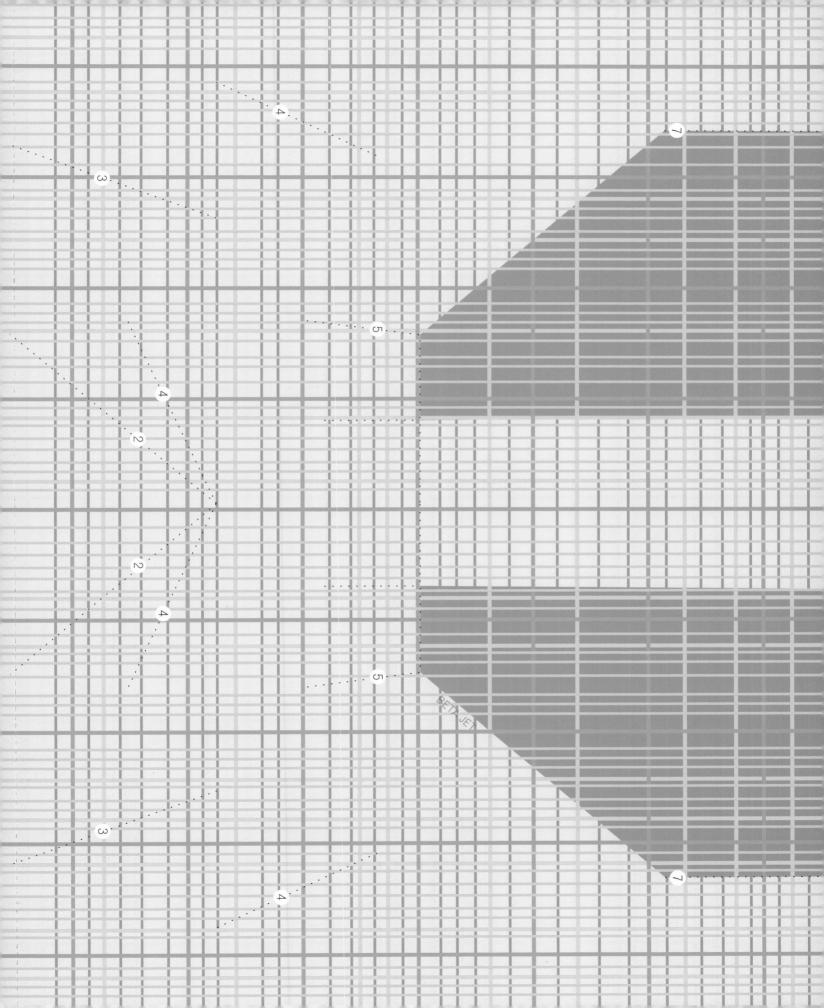

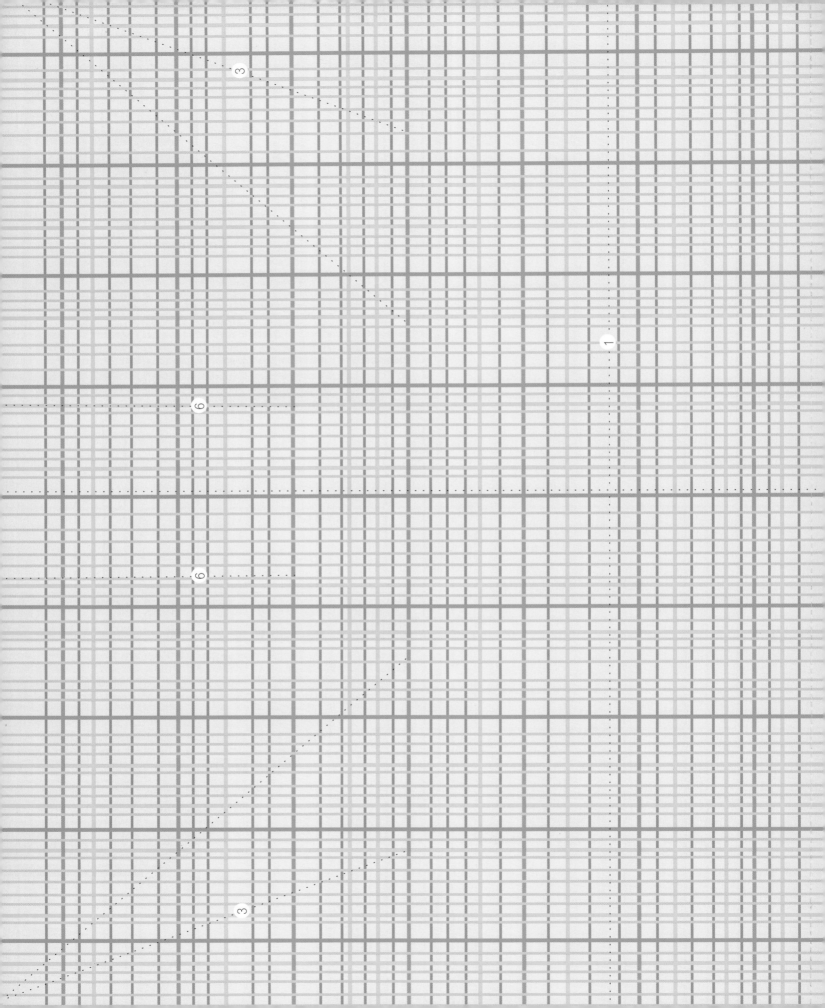

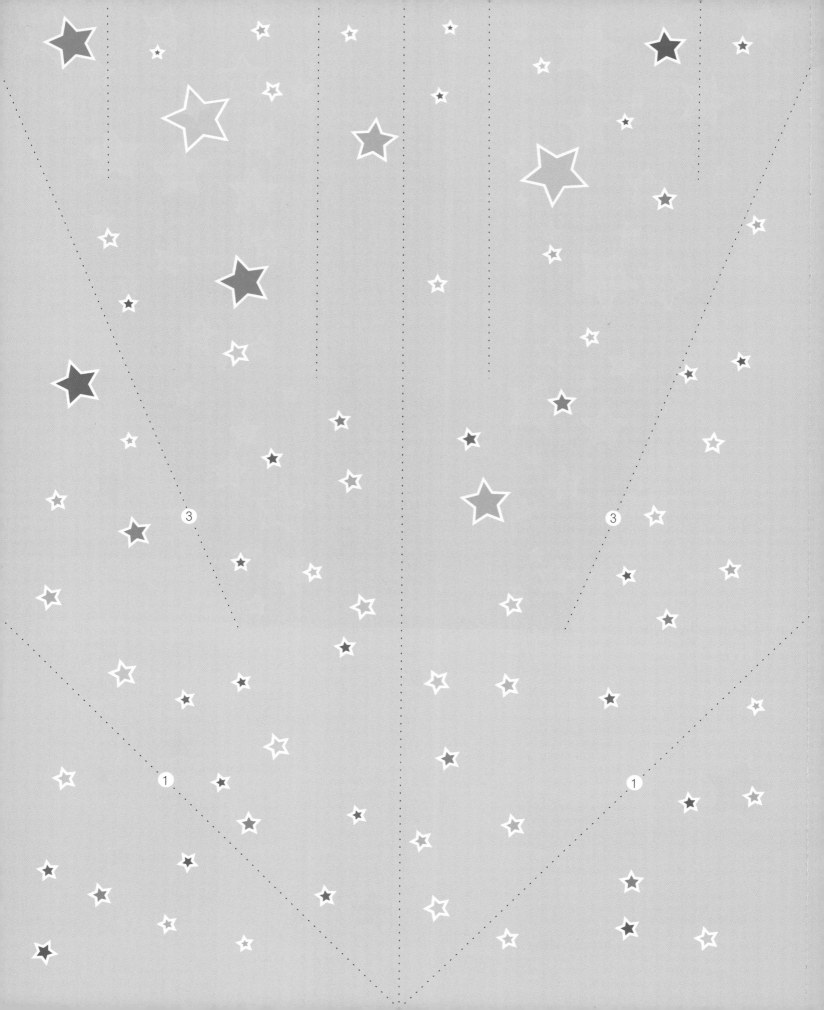

STAR SHUTTLE

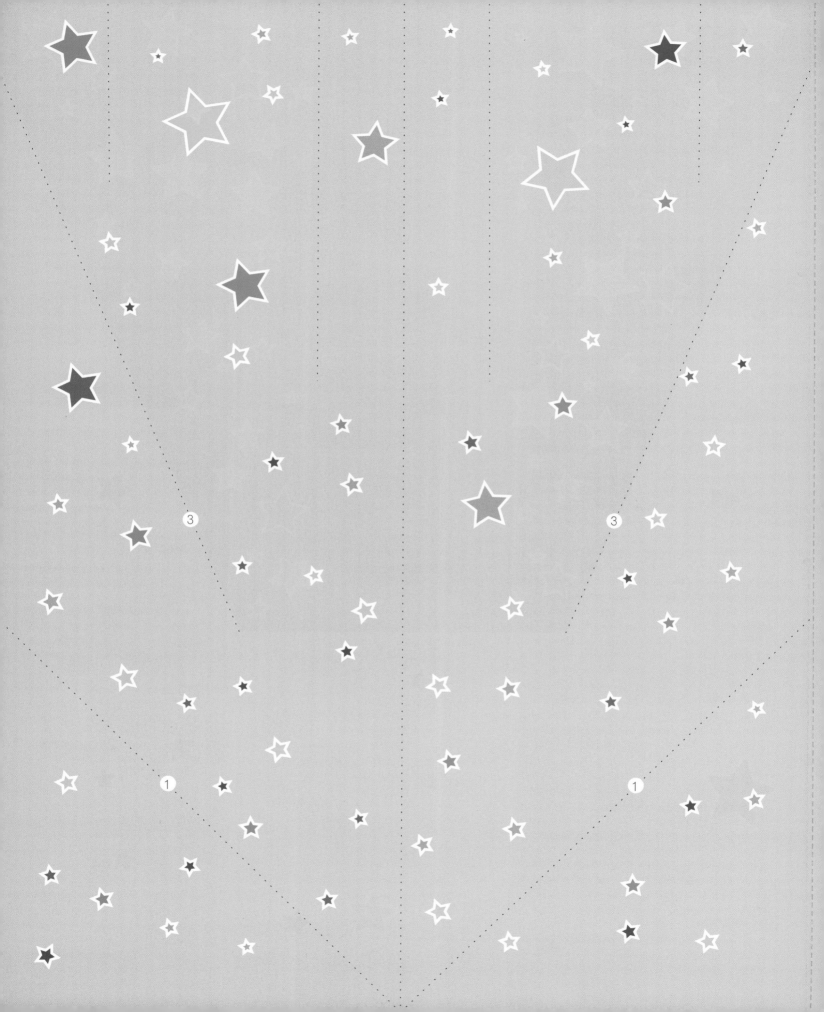

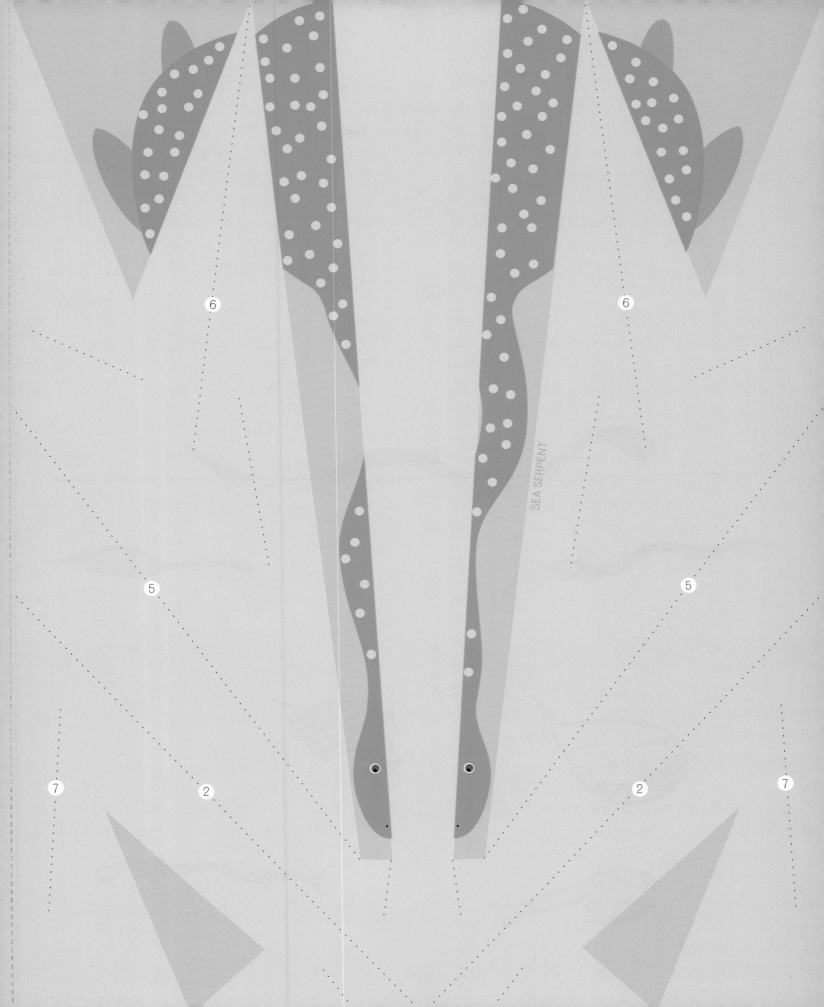

SEA SERPENT

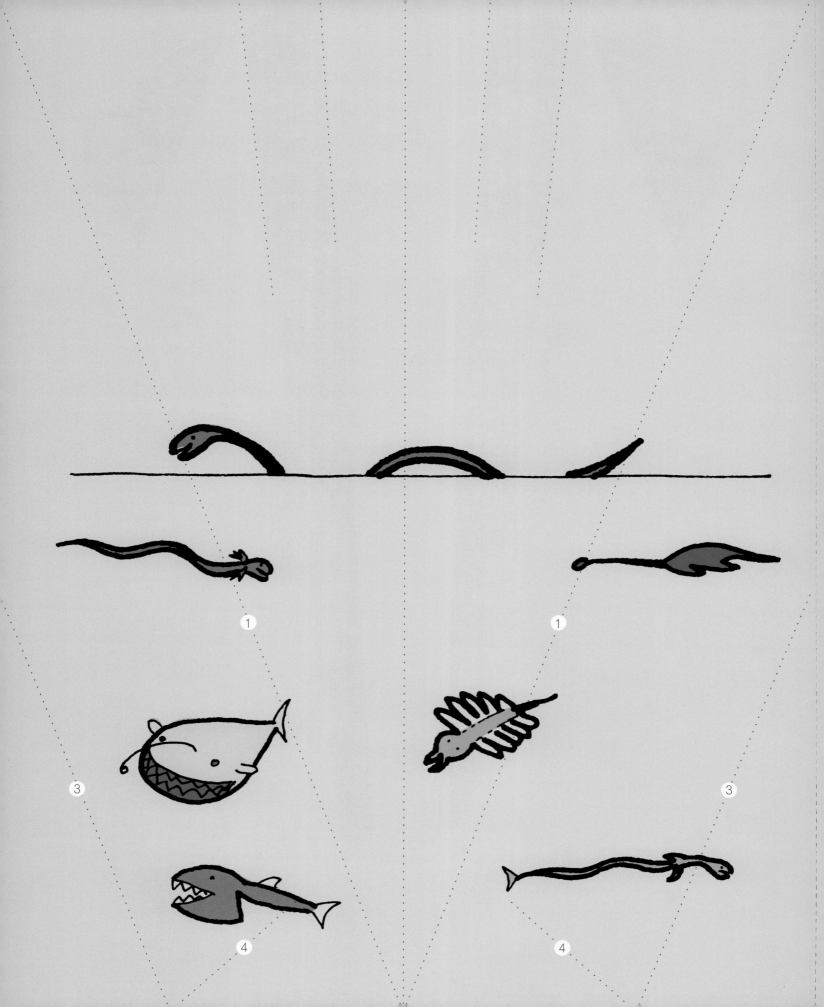

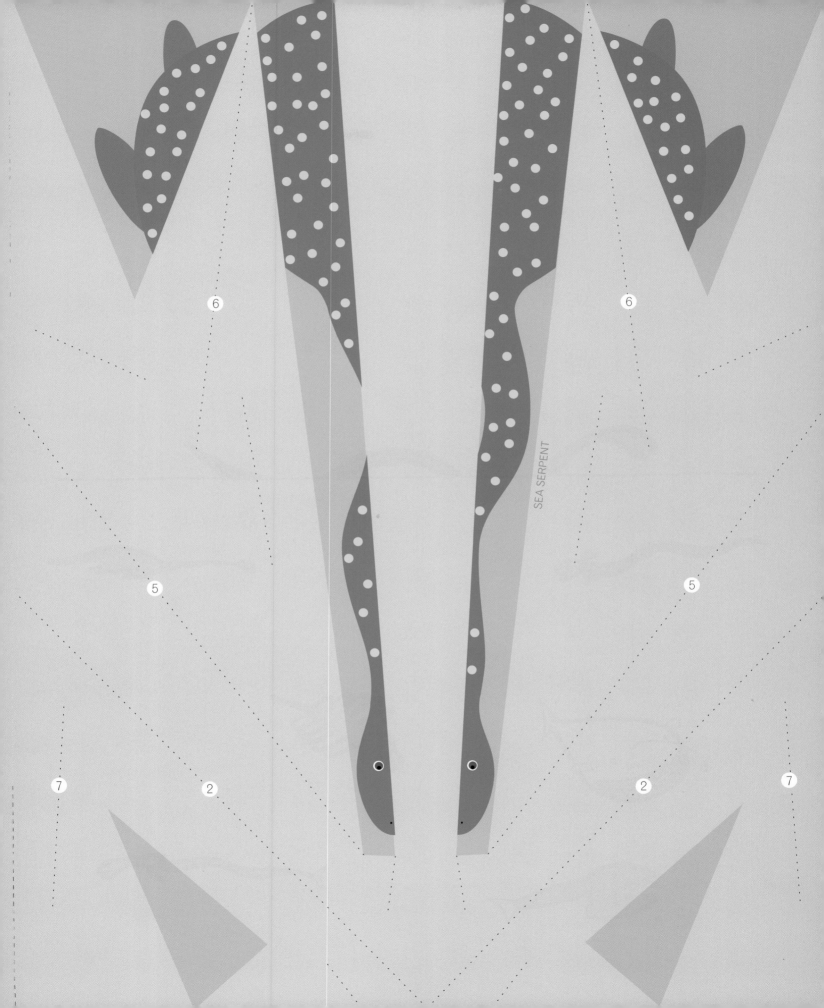

SEA SERPENT

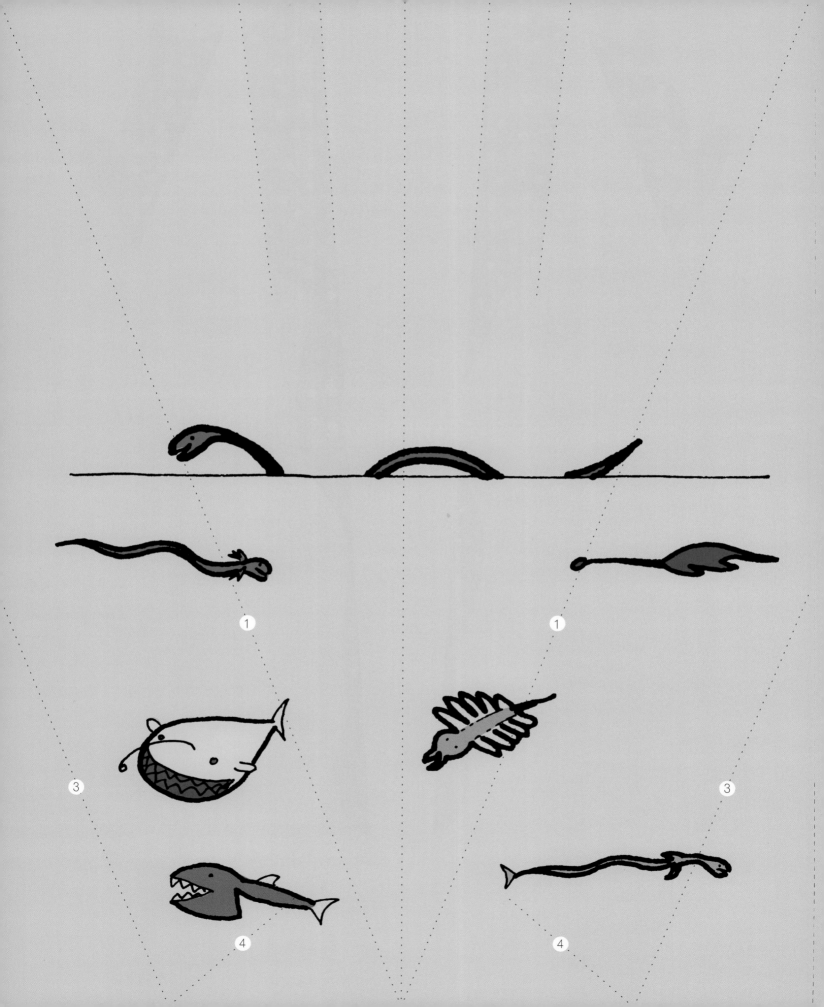

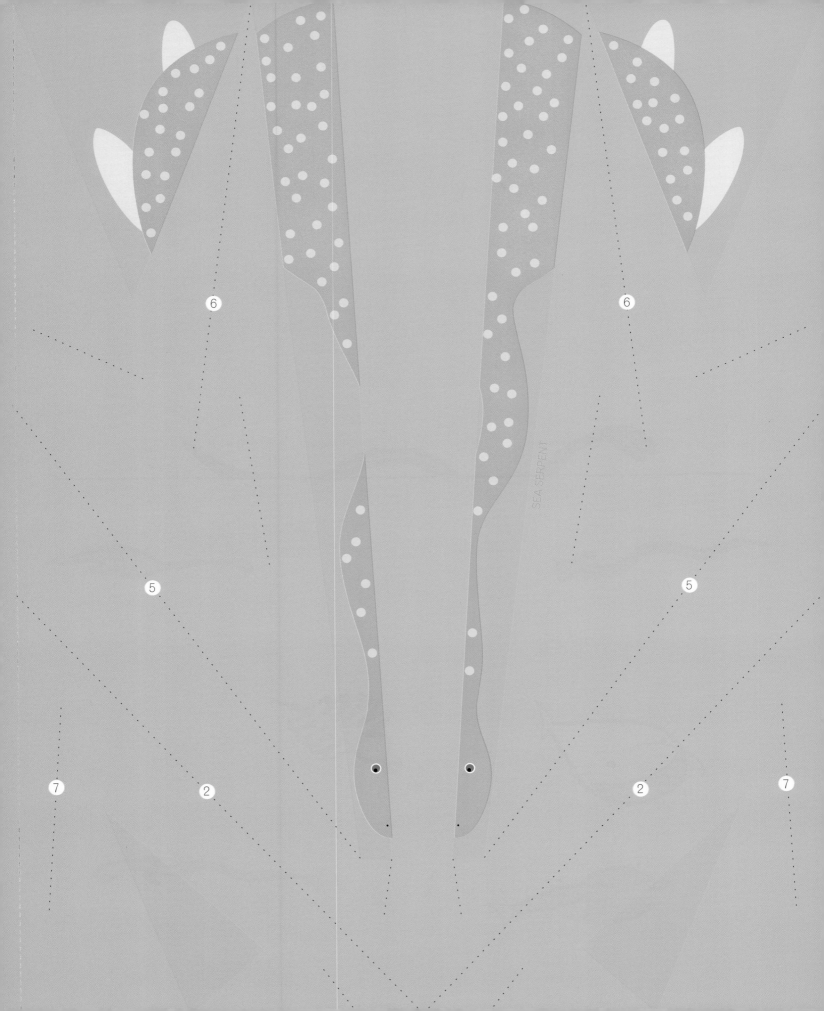

SEA SERPENT

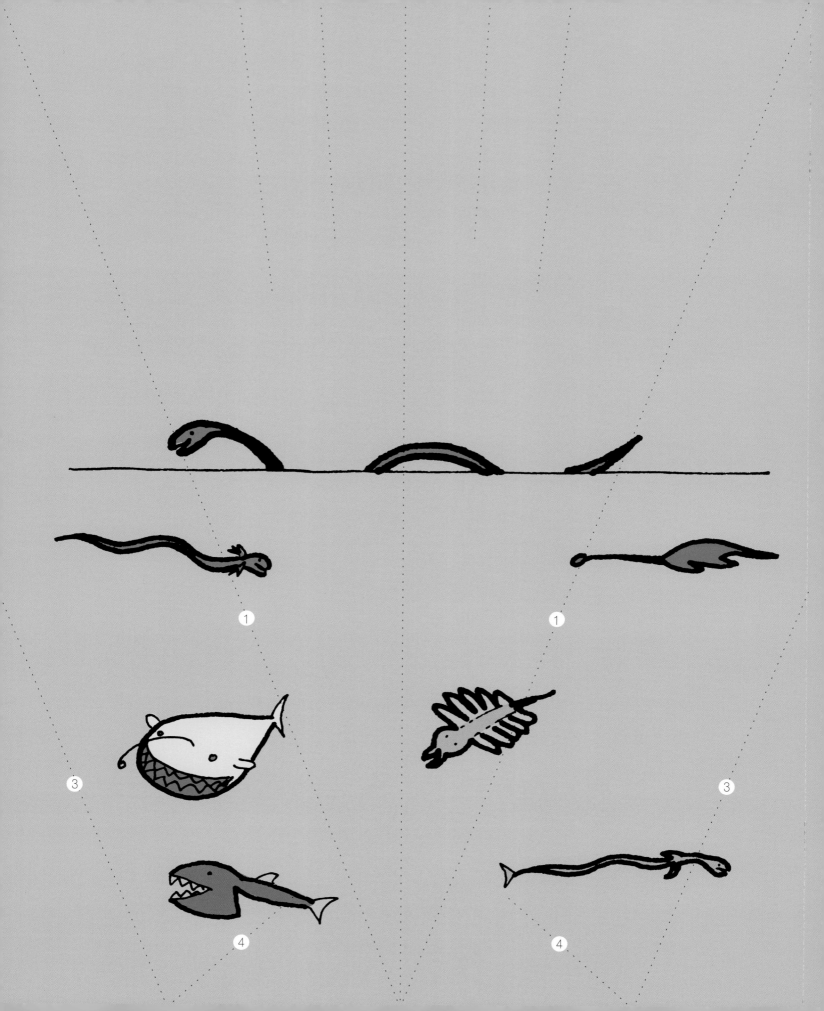

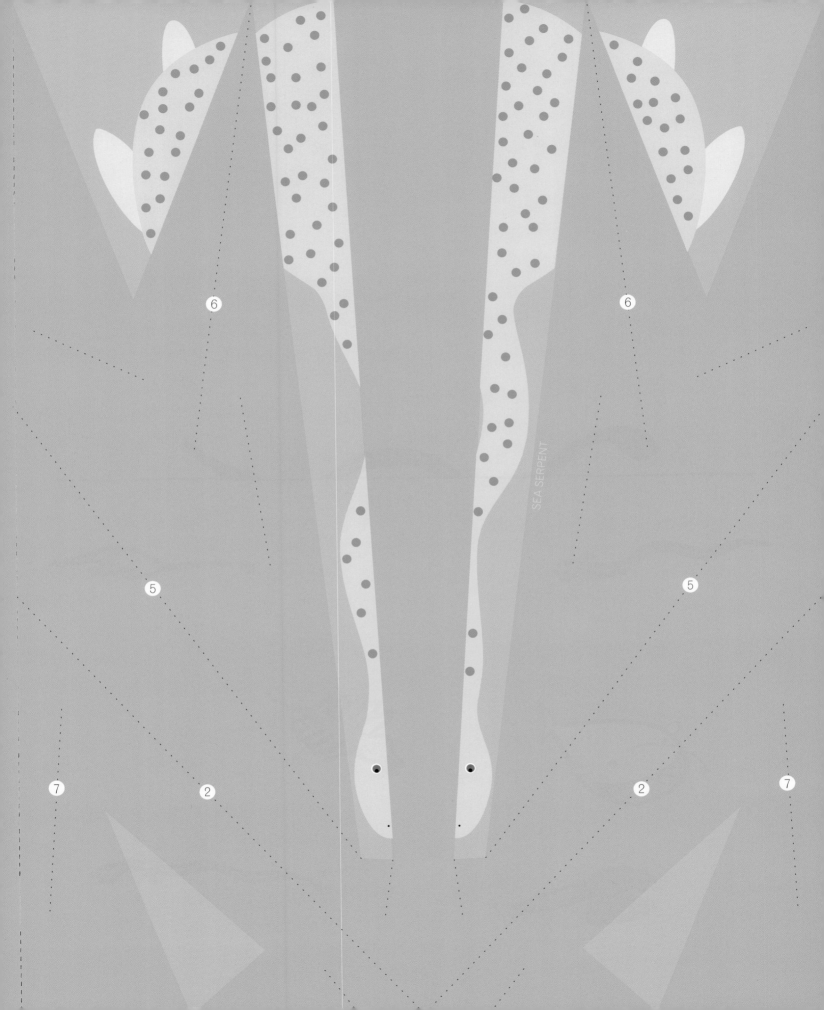

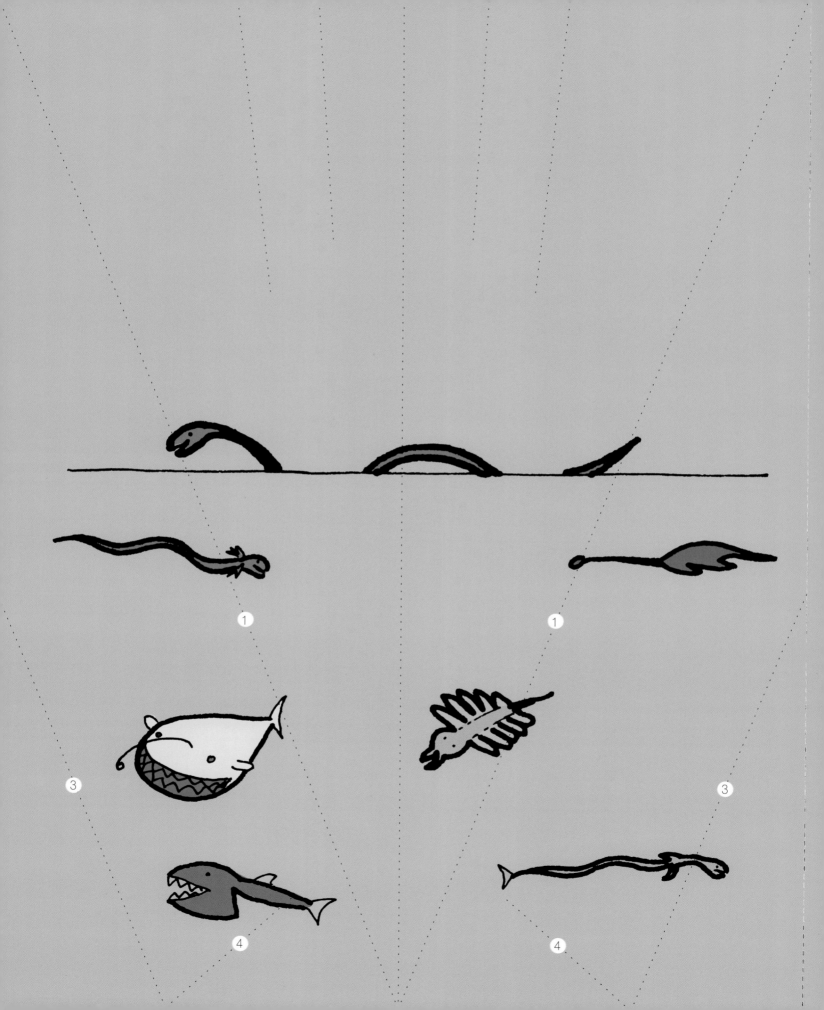

MONSTER

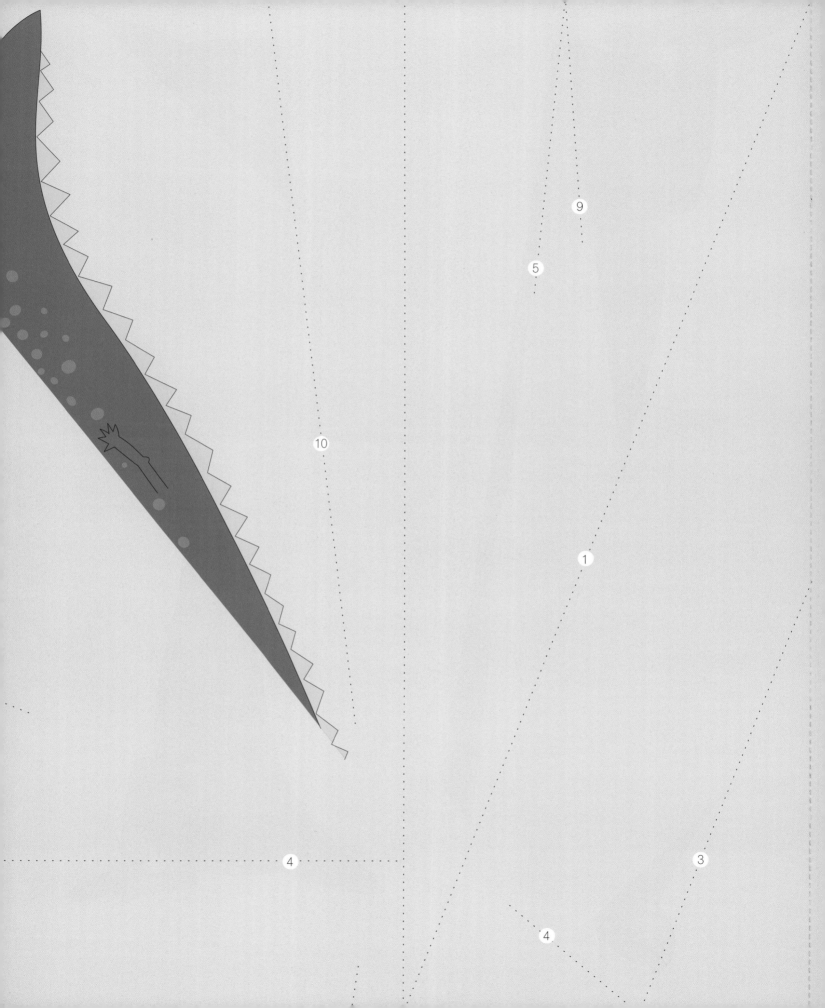

MONSTER

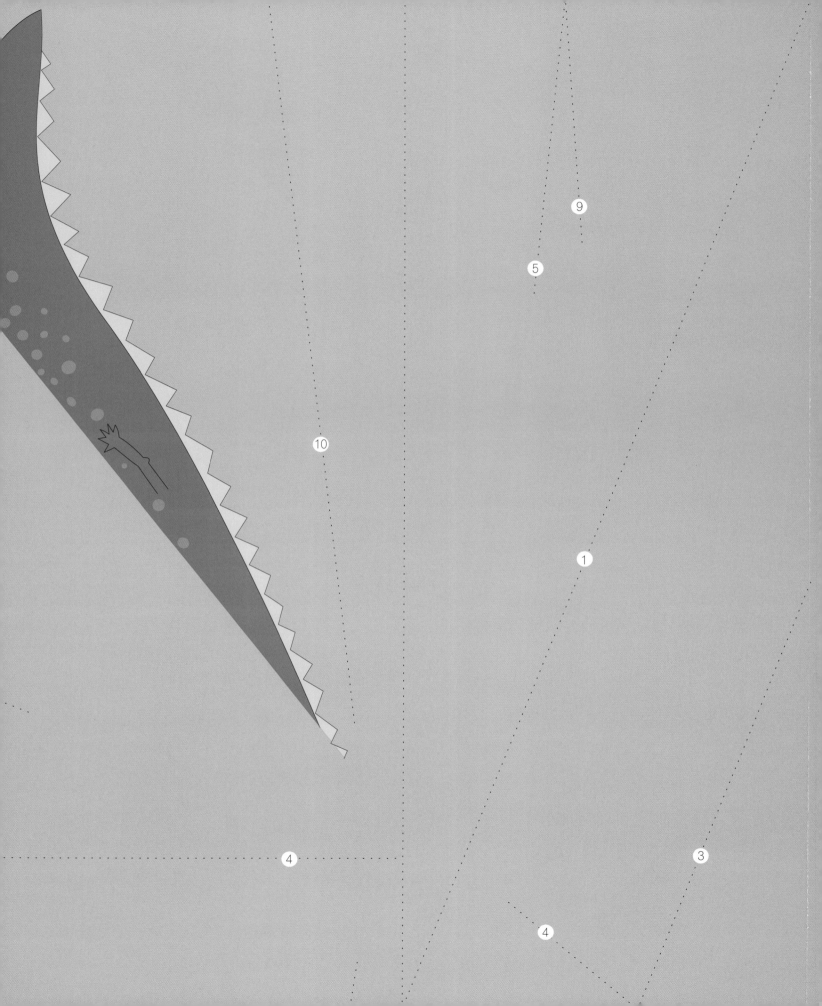

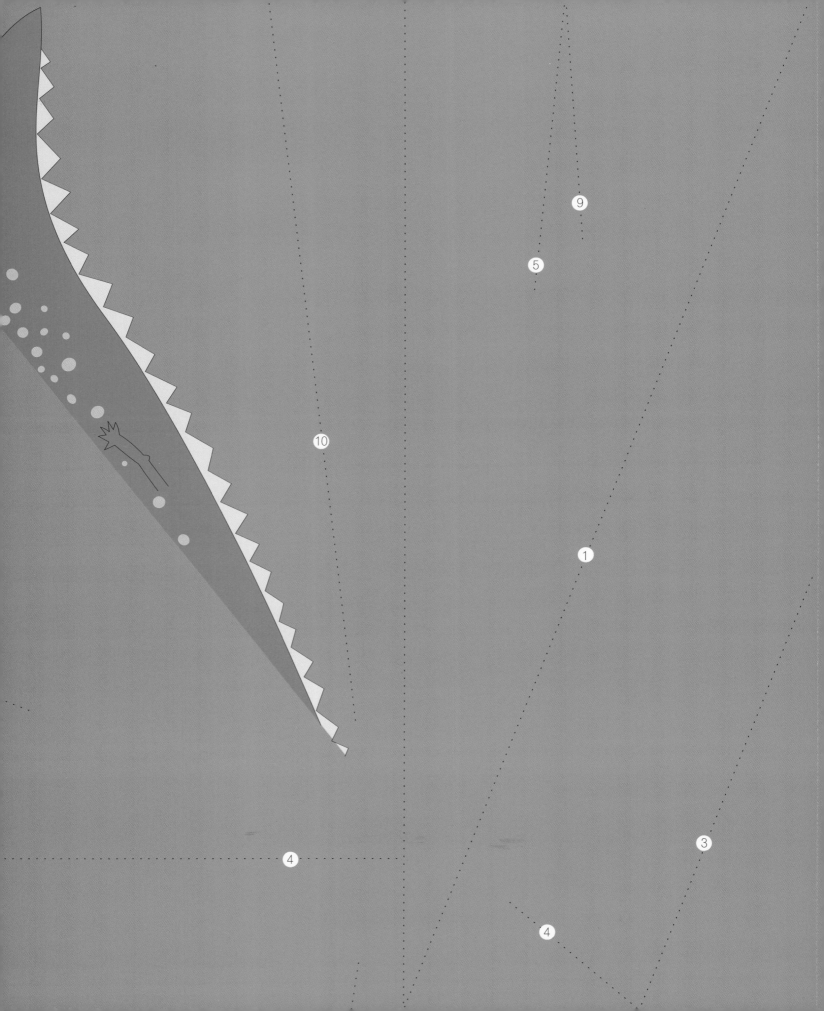

MONSTER

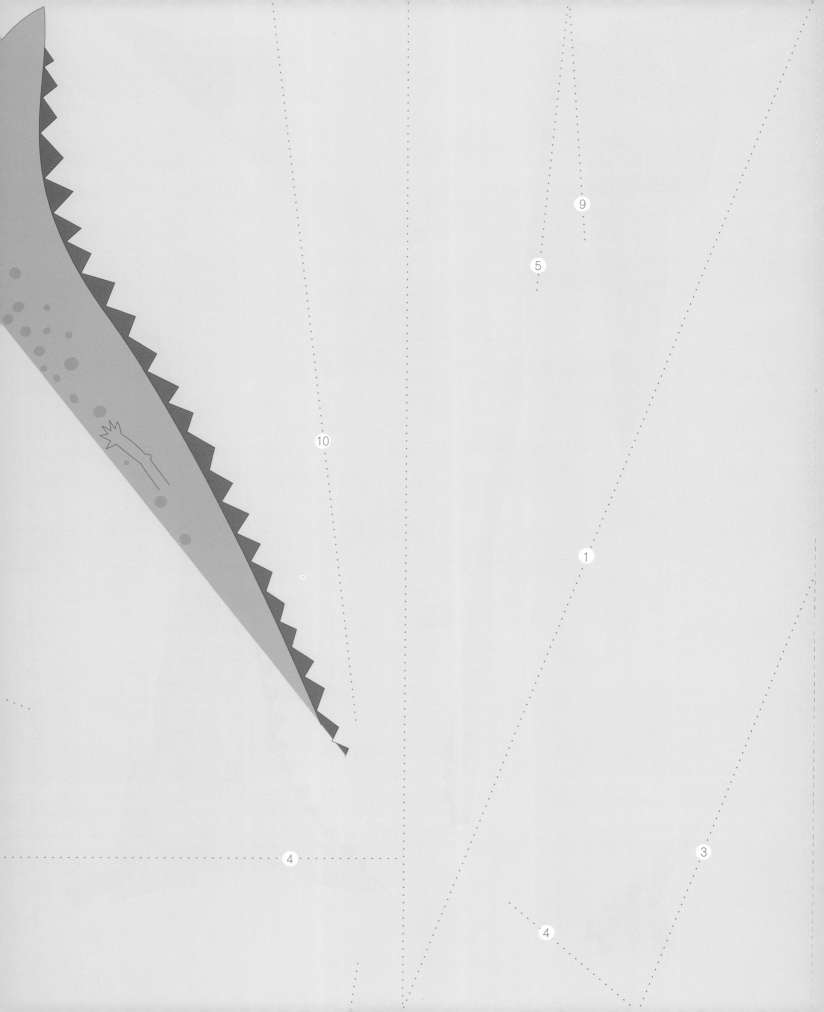

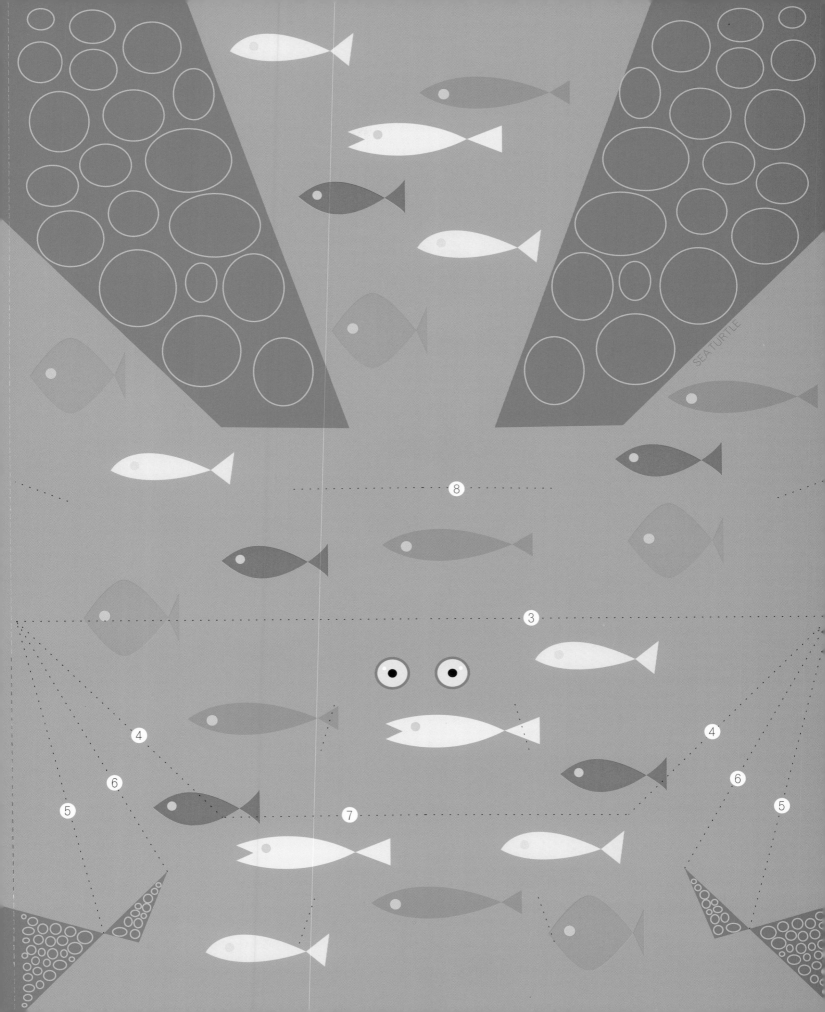

SEA TURTLE

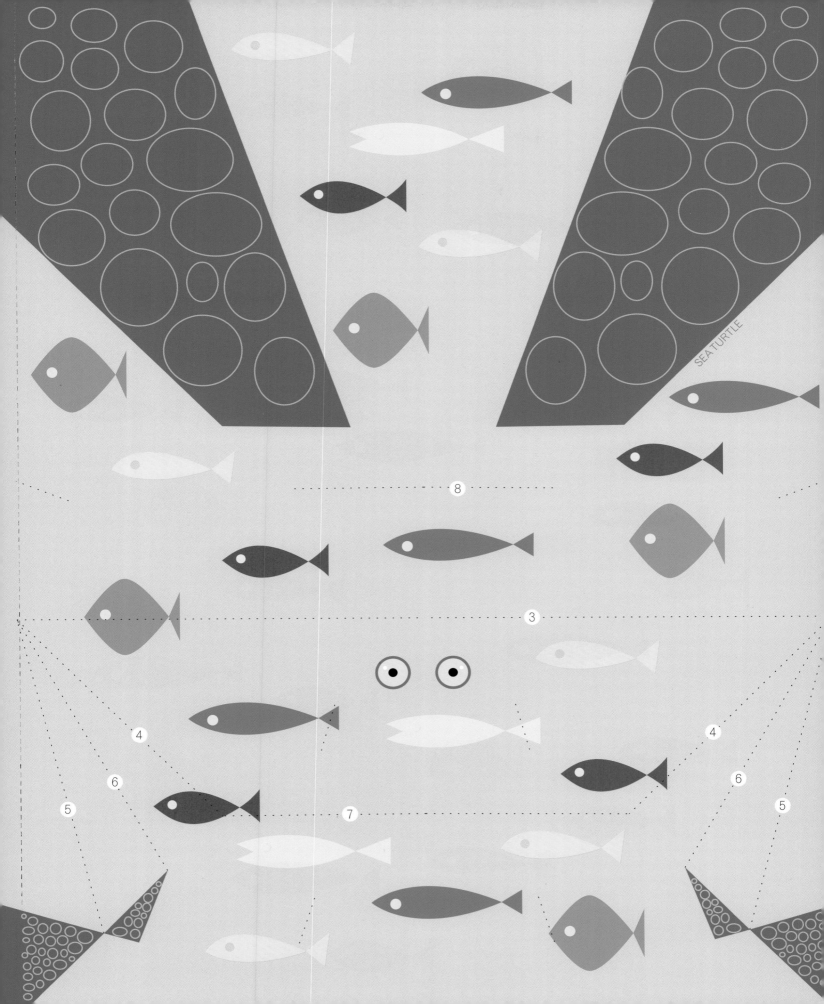

SEA TURTLE

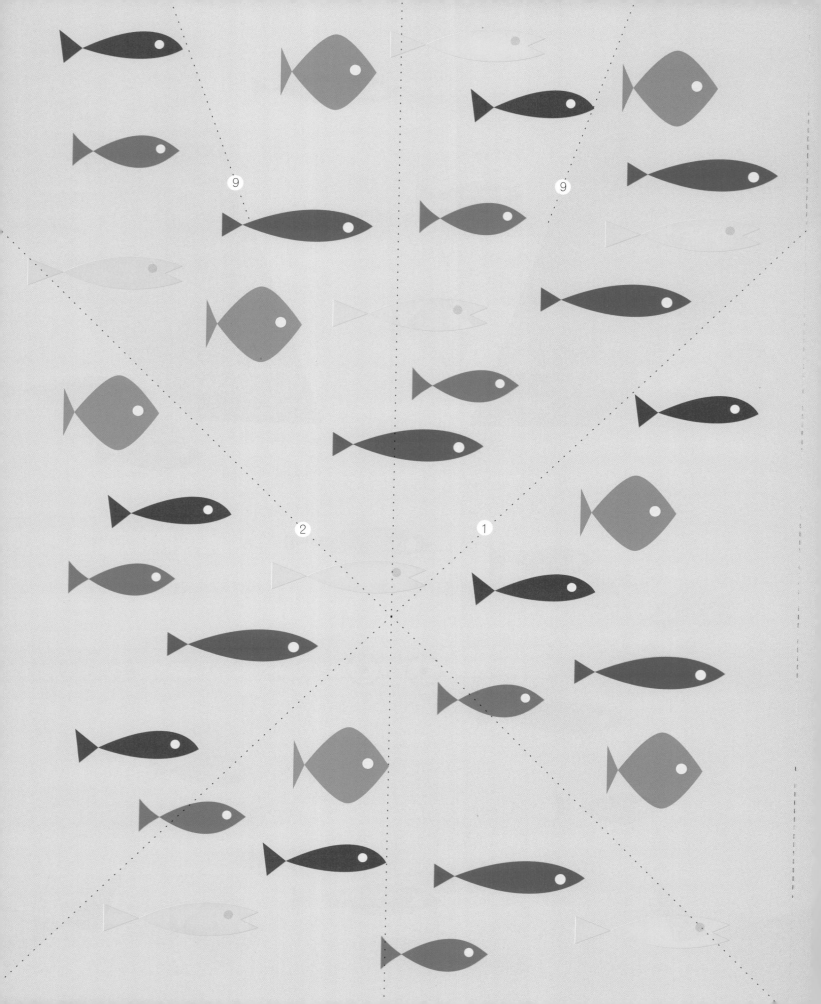

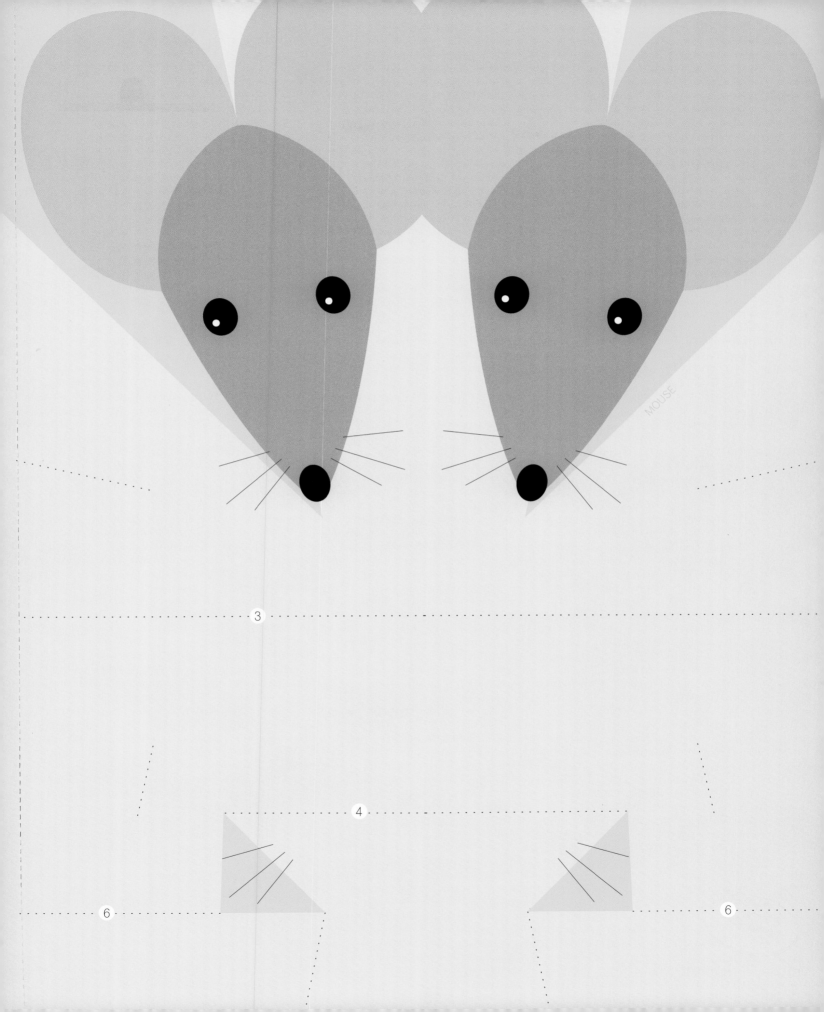

MOUSE

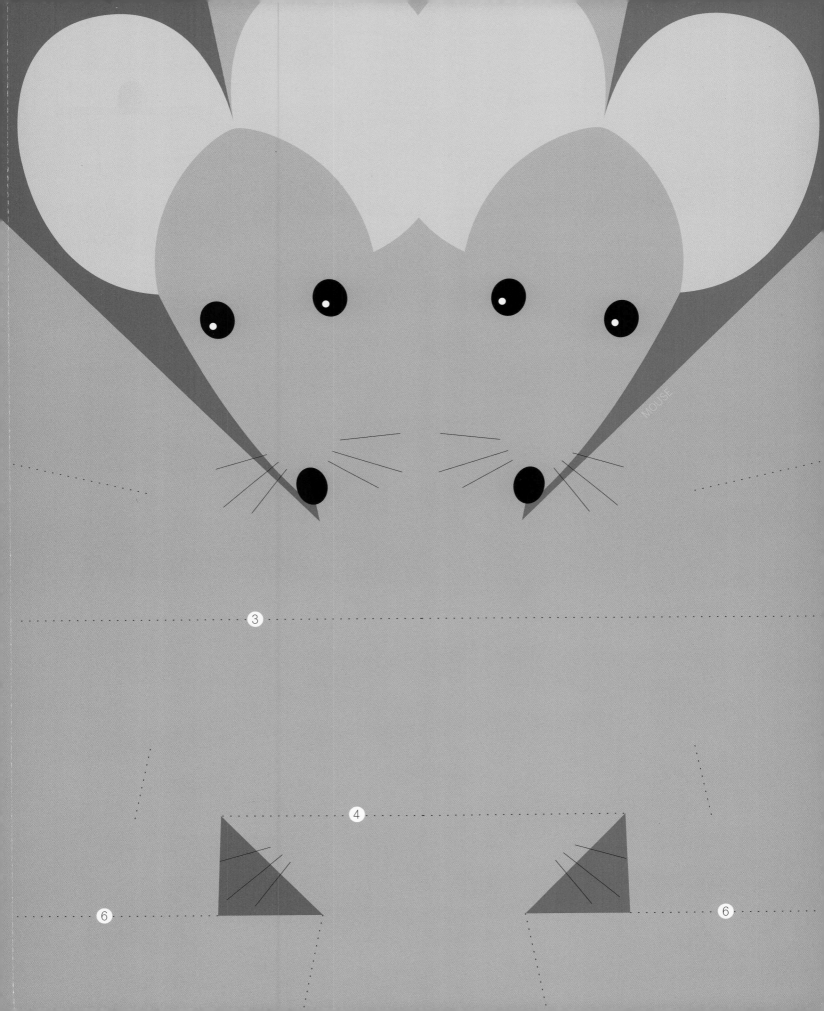

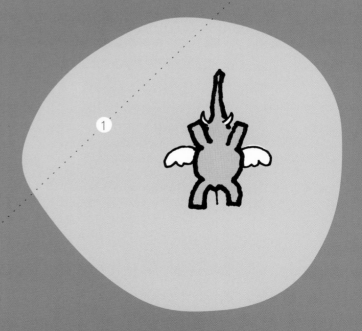

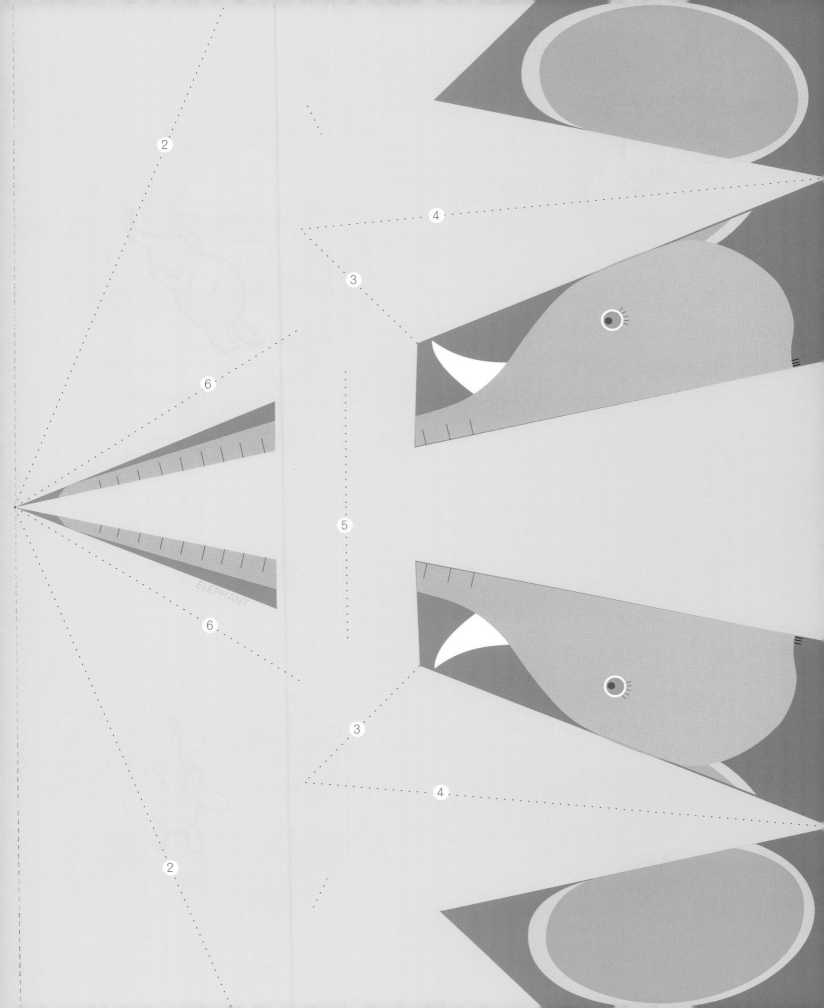

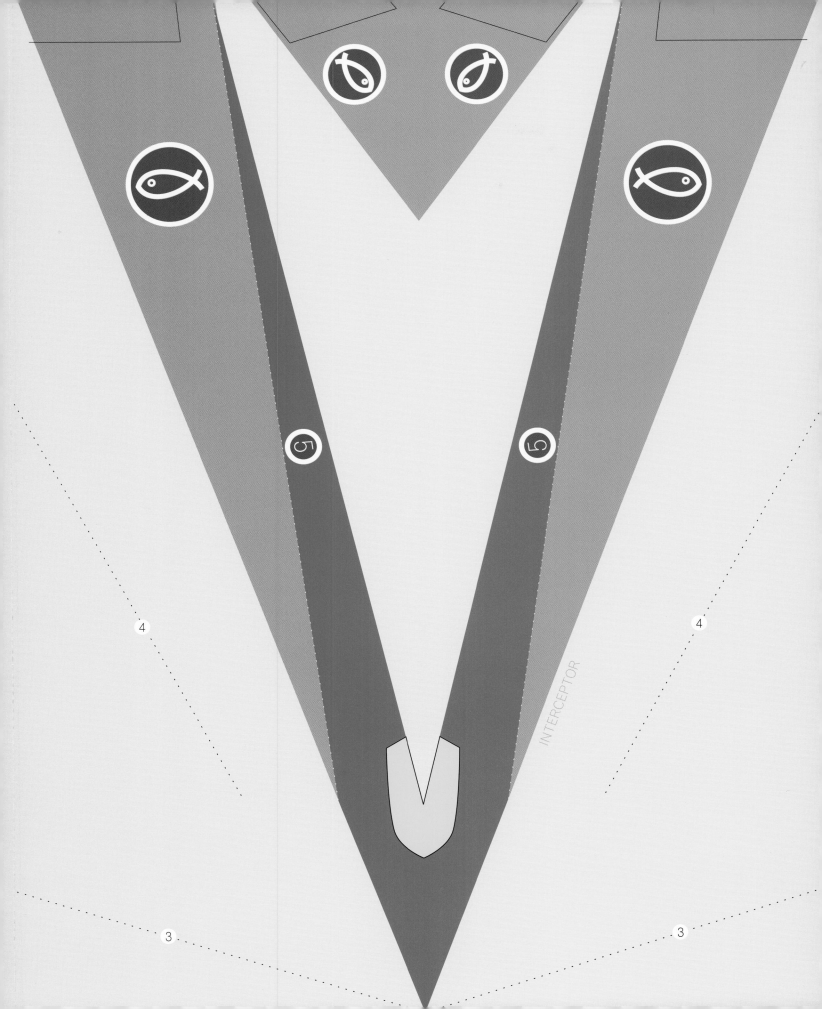

INTERCEPTOR

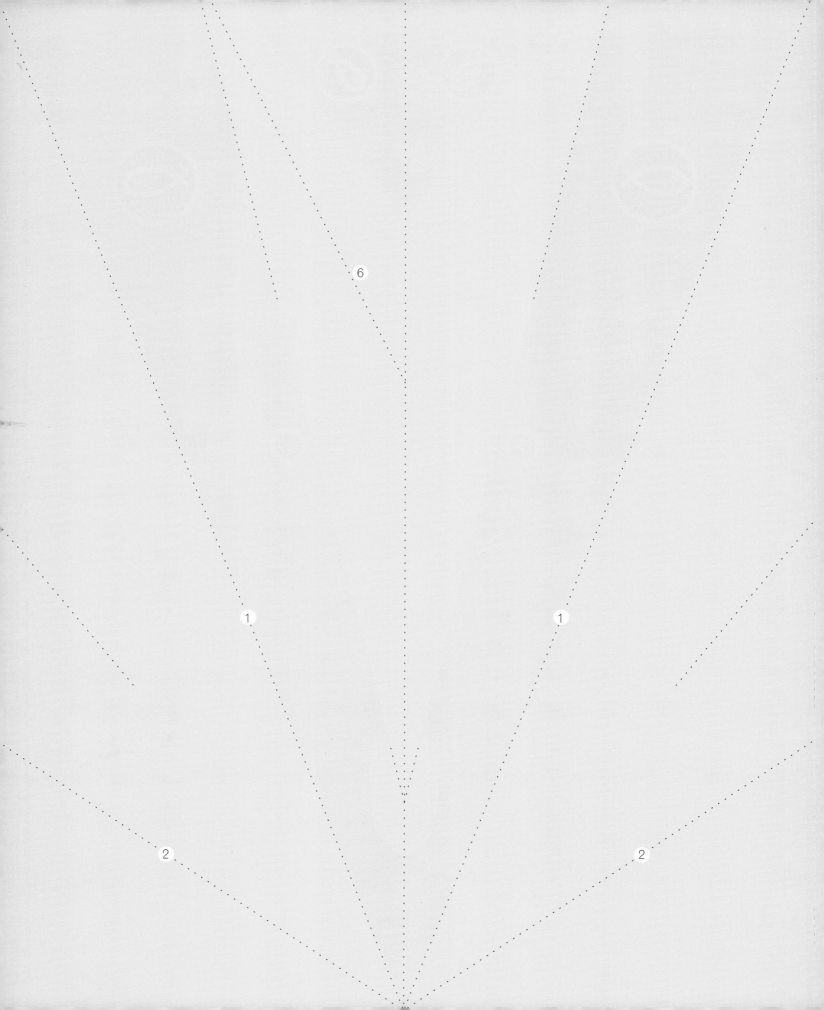

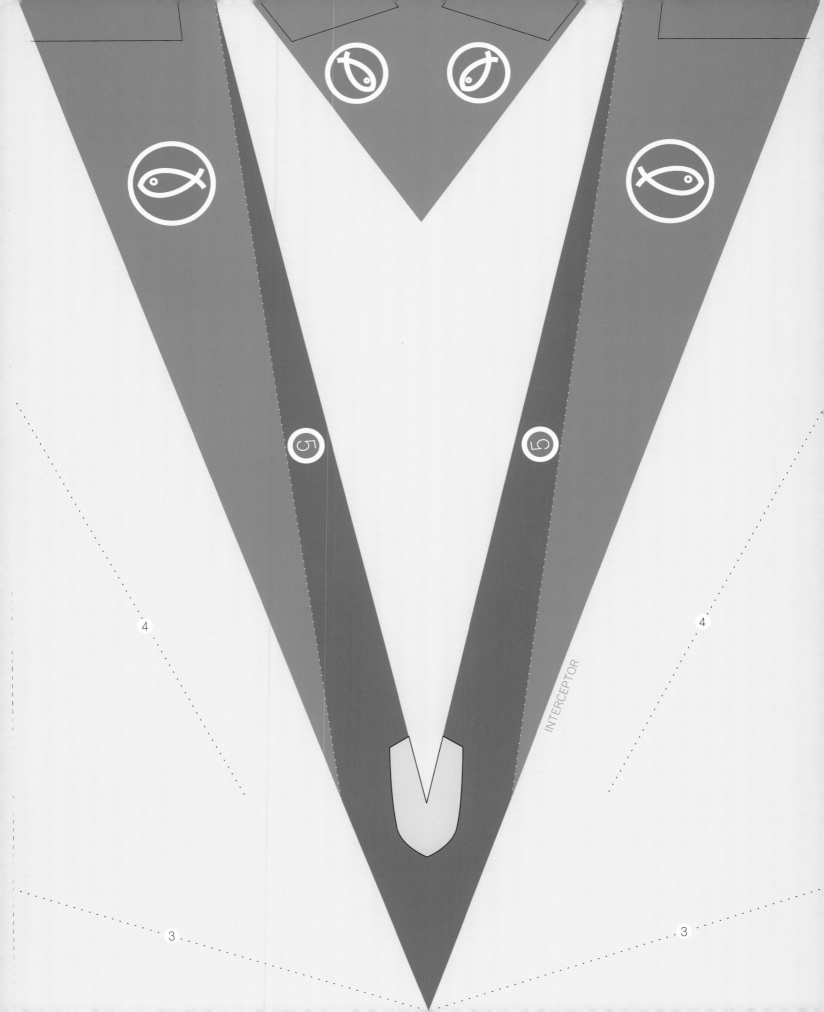

INTERCEPTOR

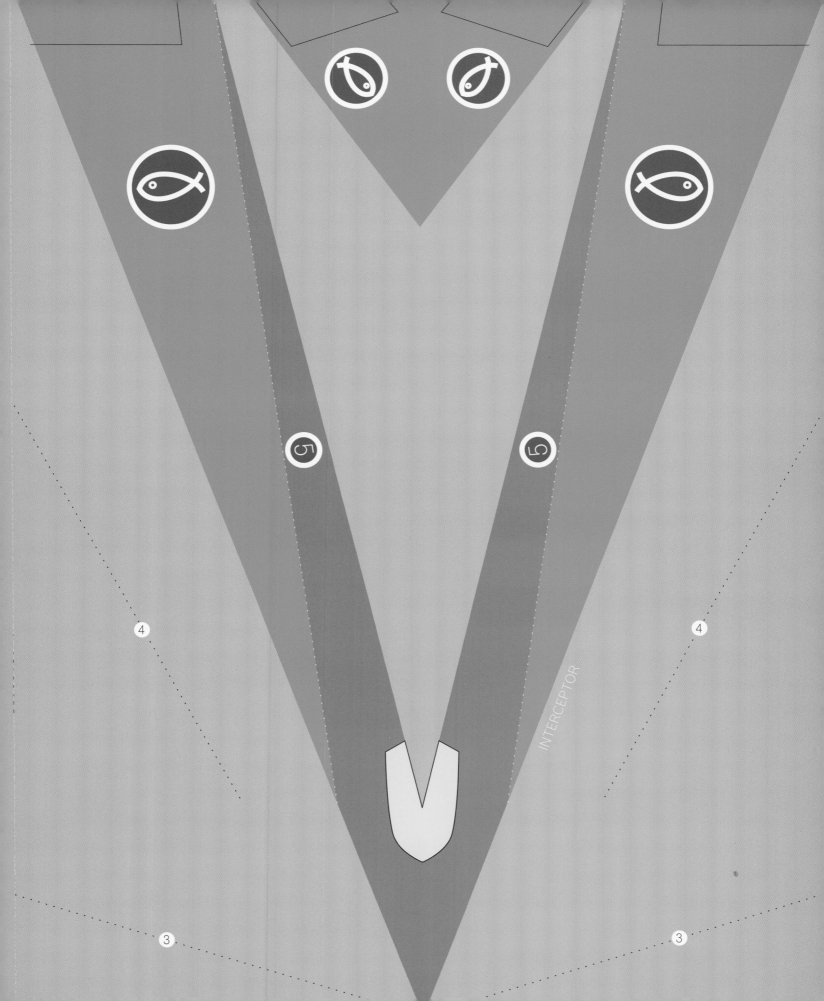

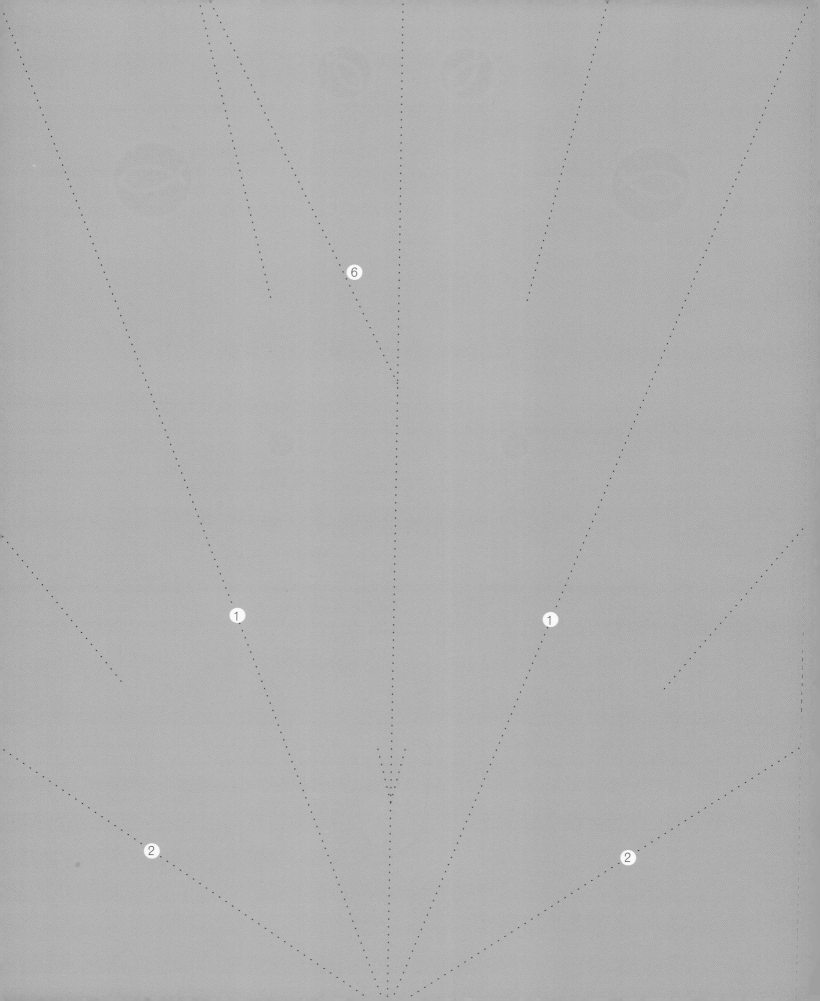

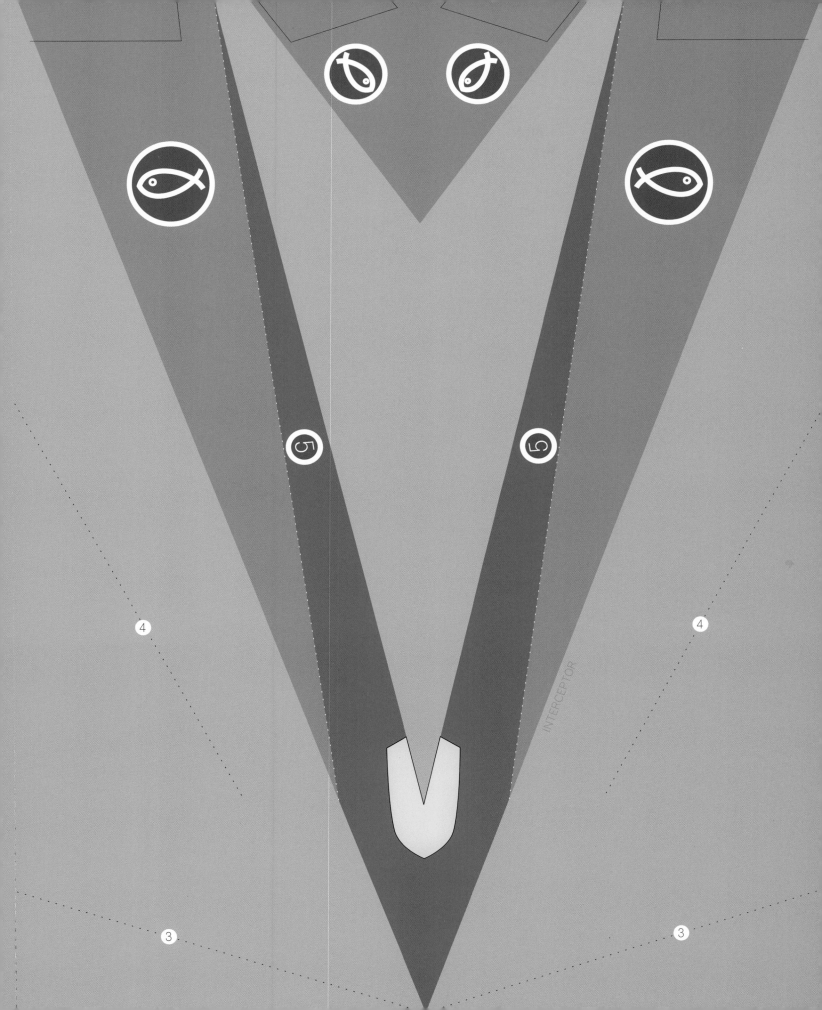

VALKYRIE

North American XB-70 Valkyrie

1

1

VALKYRIE

North American XB-70 Valkyrie

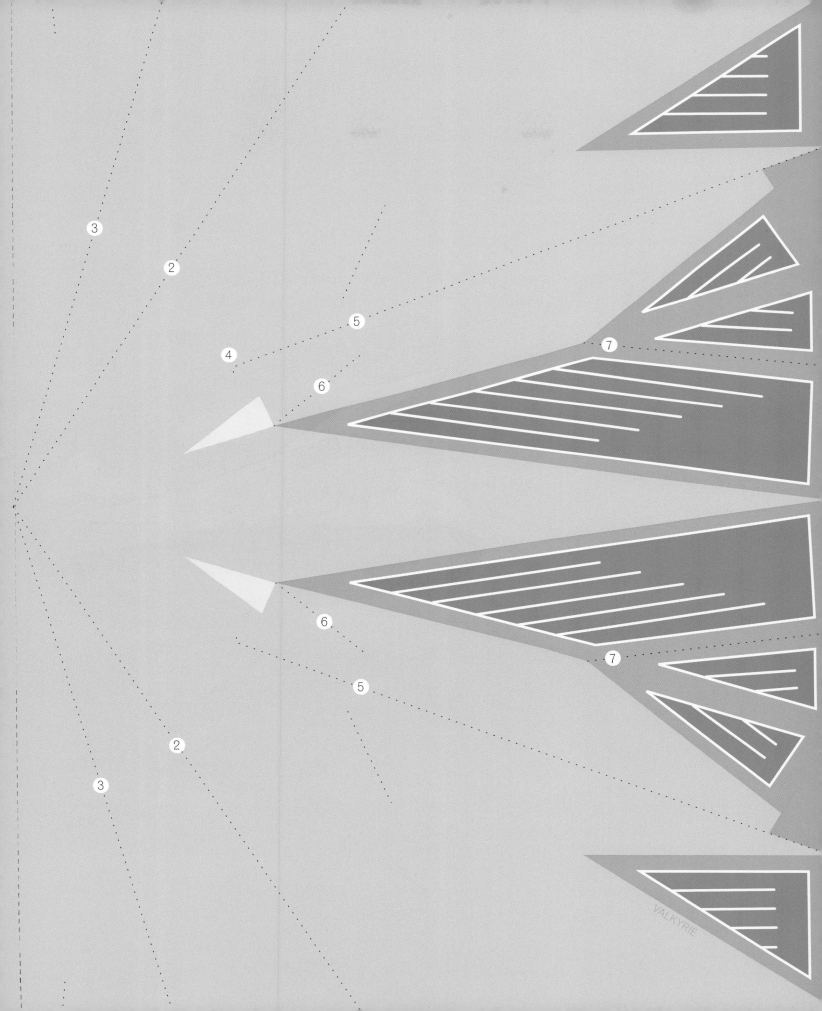

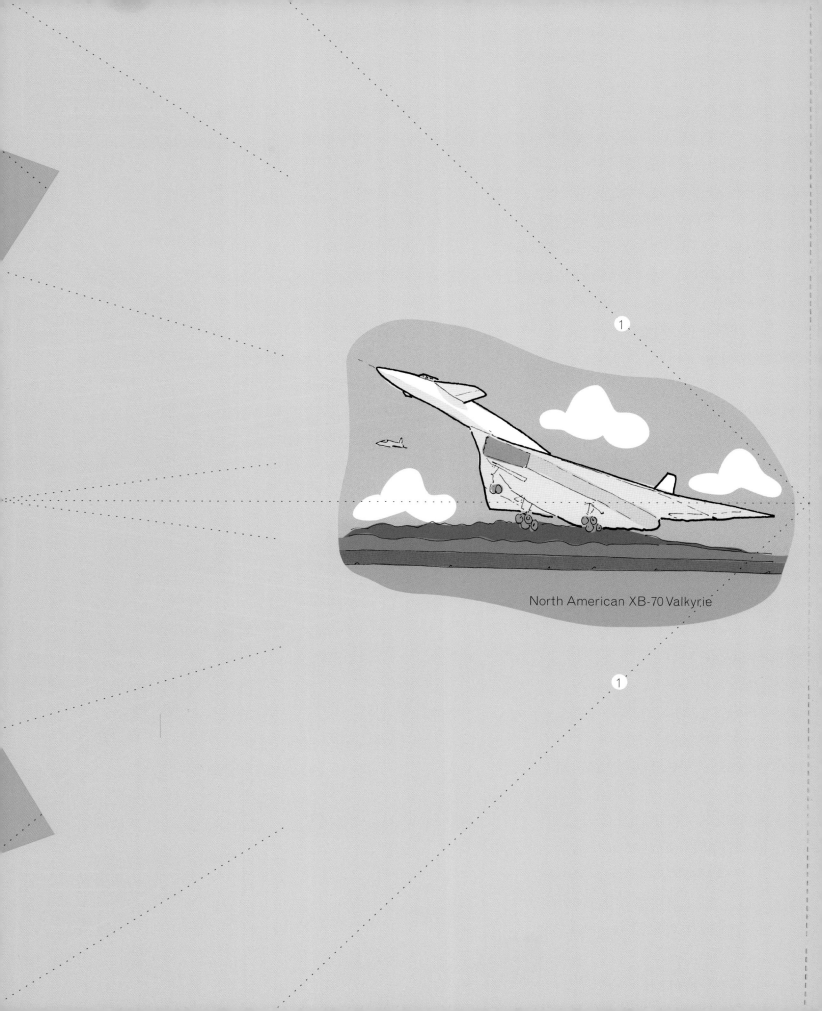

North American XB-70 Valkyrie

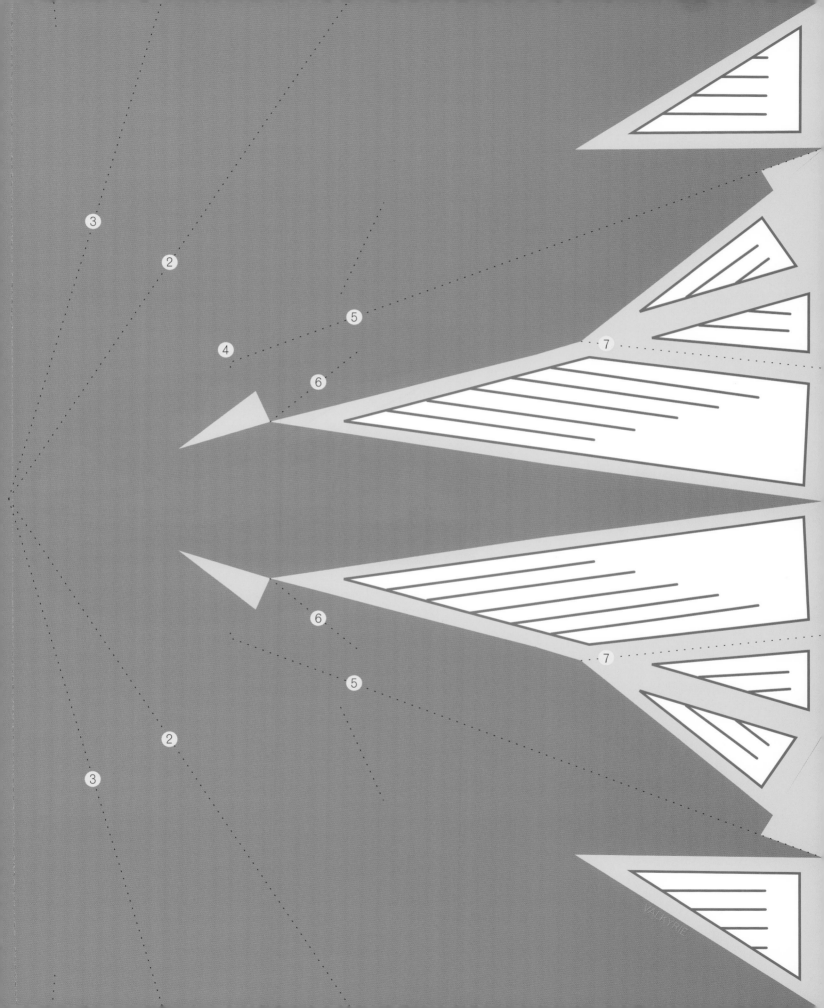

North American XB-70 Valkyrie

1

VALKYRIE

North American XB-70 Valkyrie

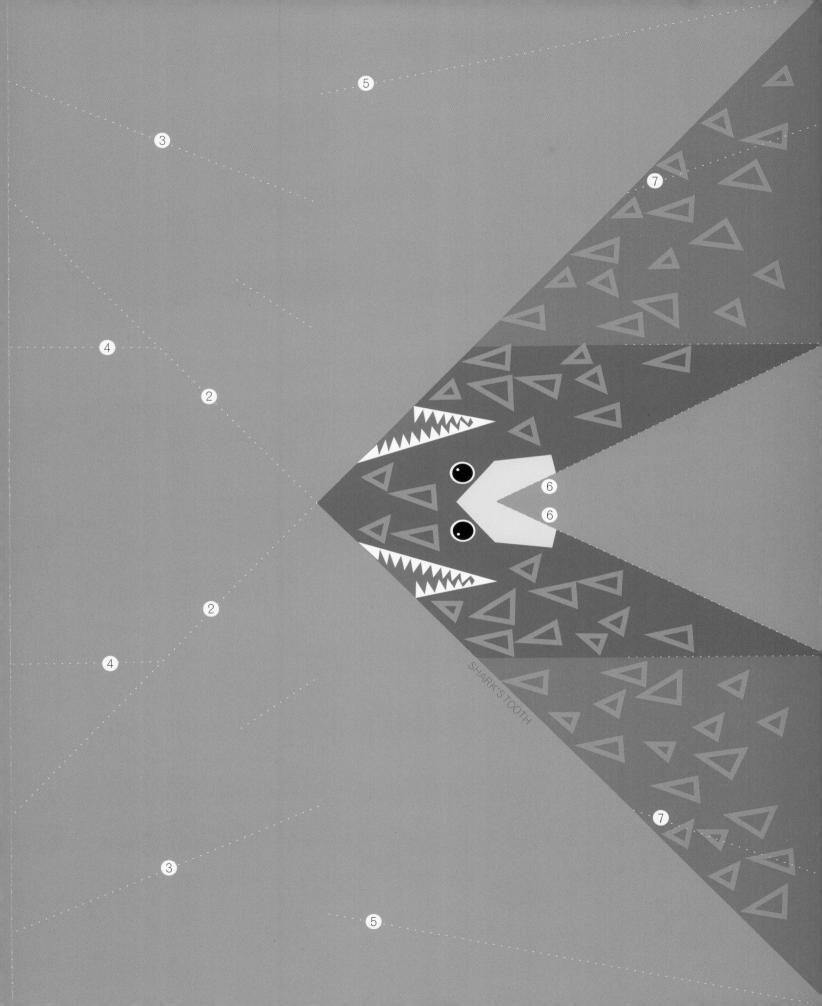

SHARK'S TOOTH

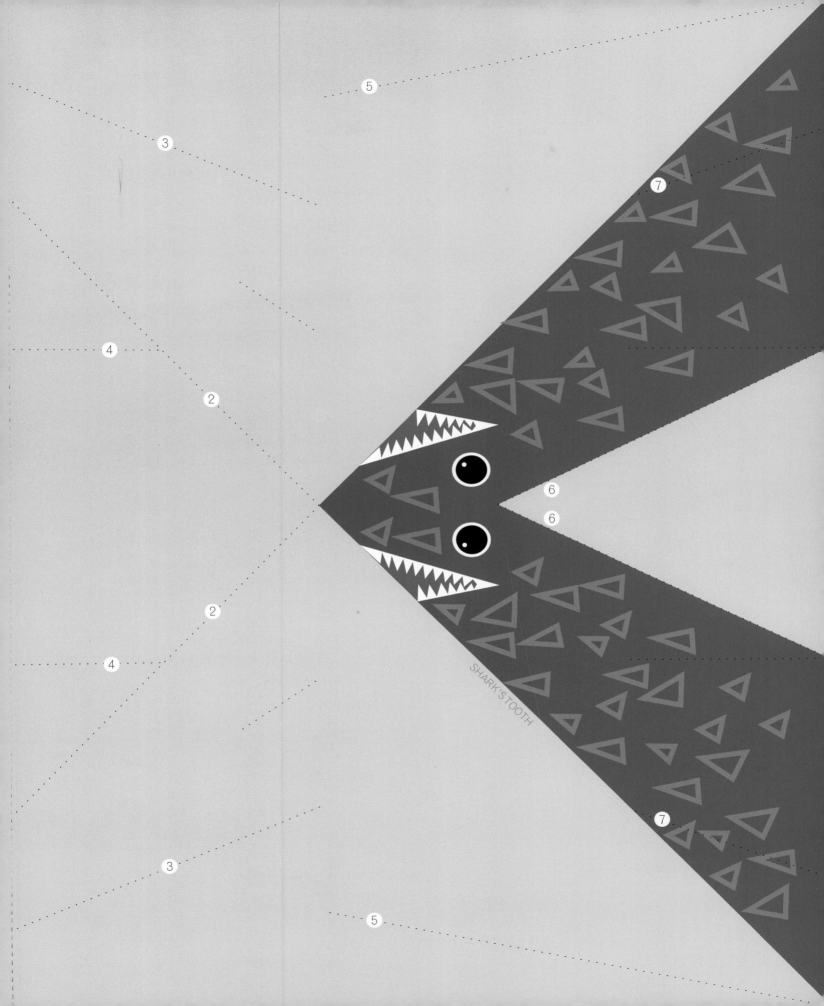

SHARK'S TOOTH

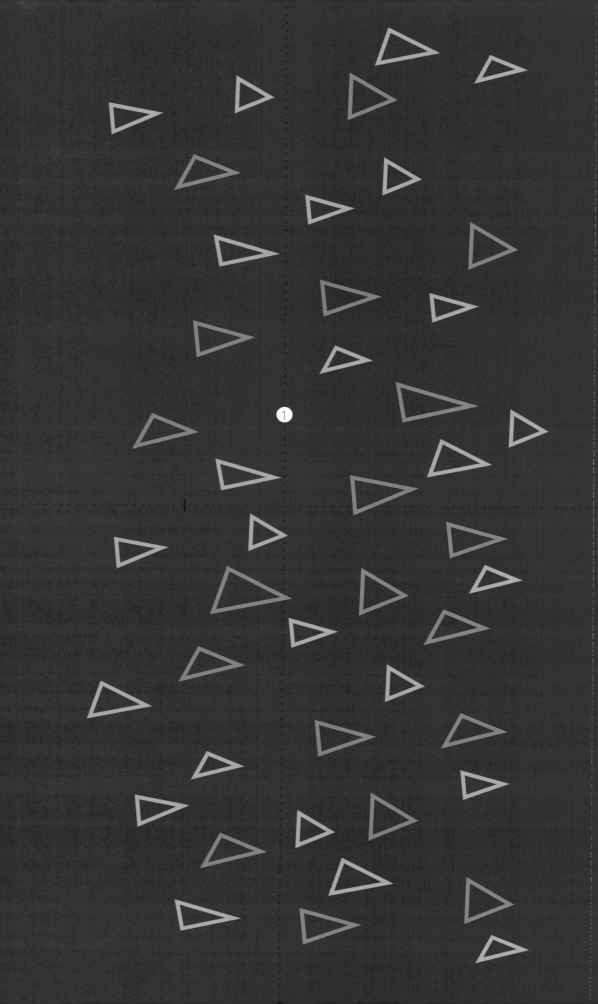

SHARK'S TOOTH

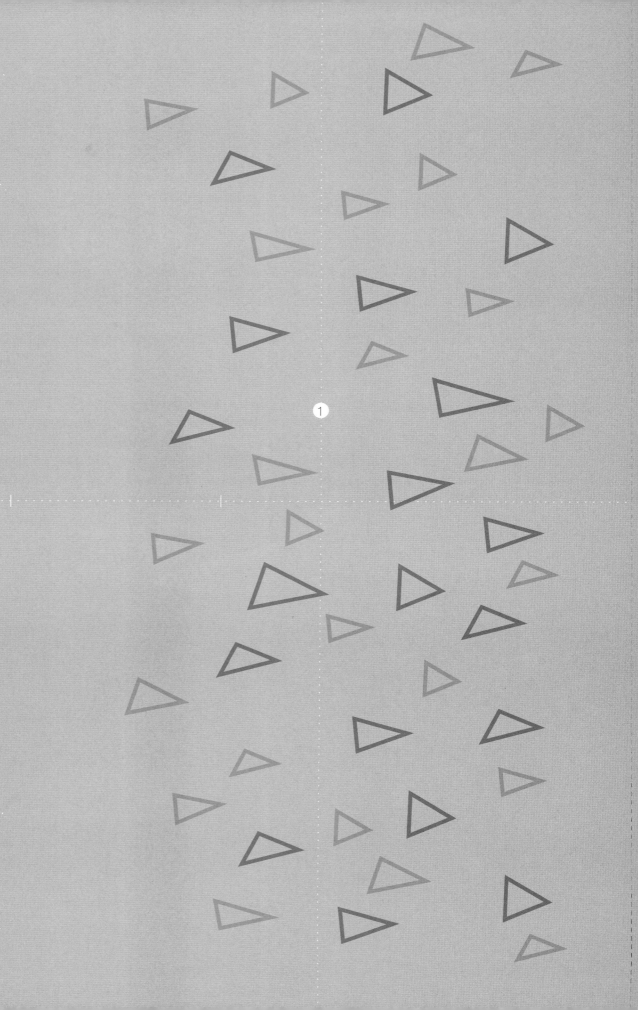

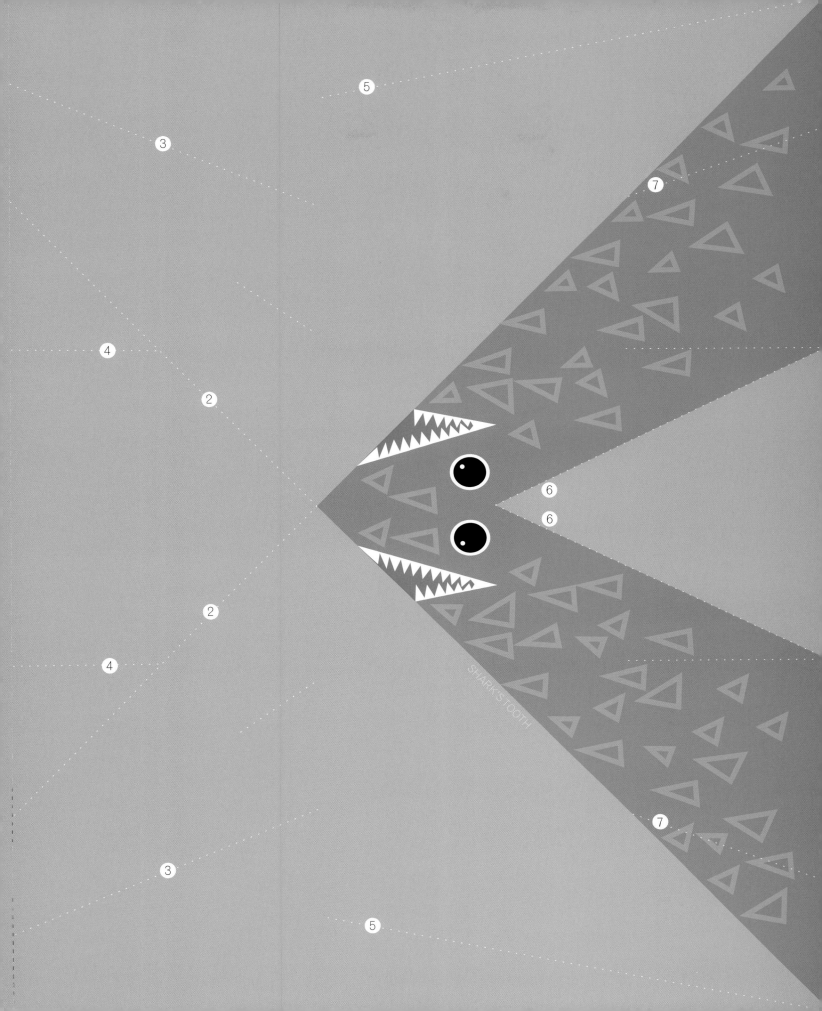

SHARK'S TOOTH

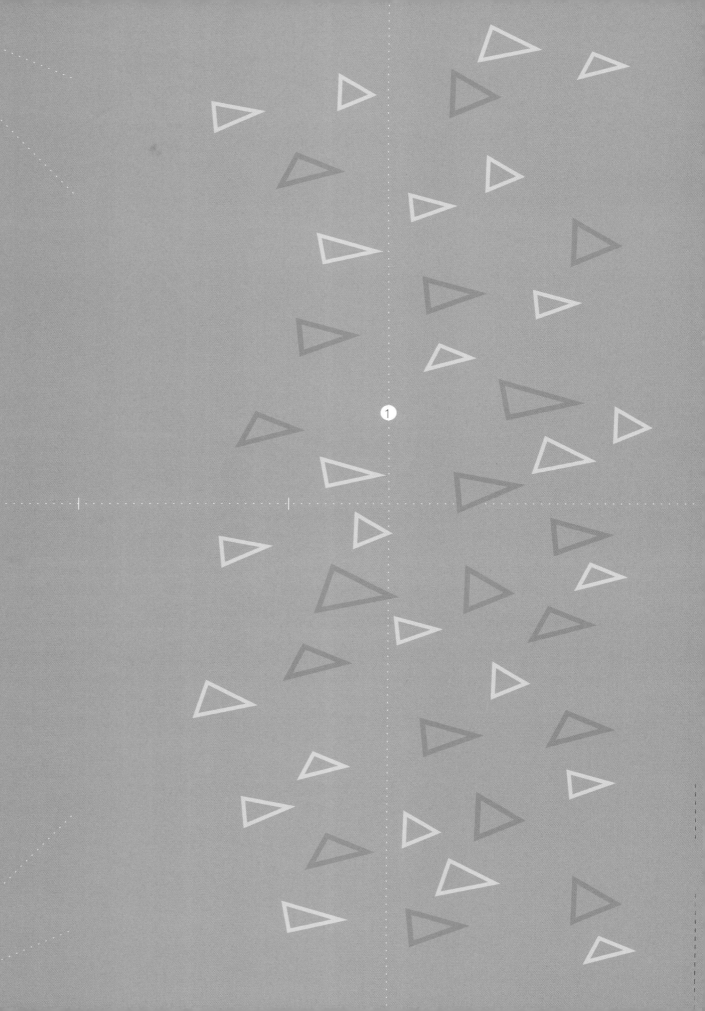

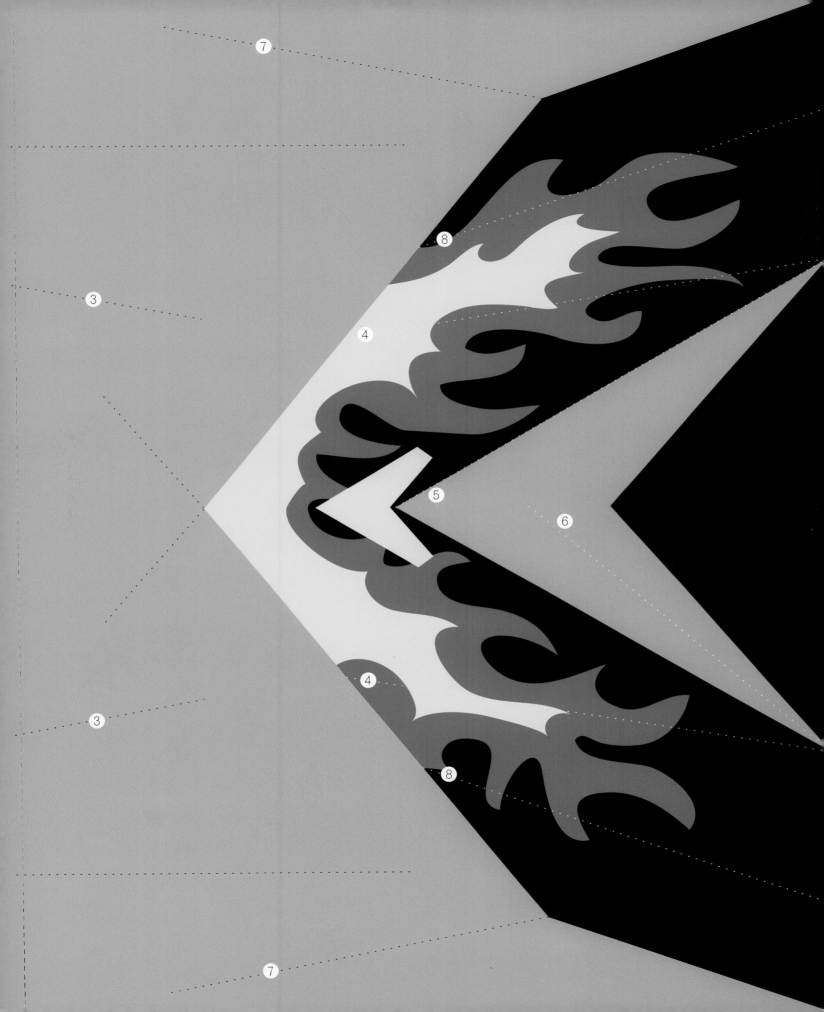

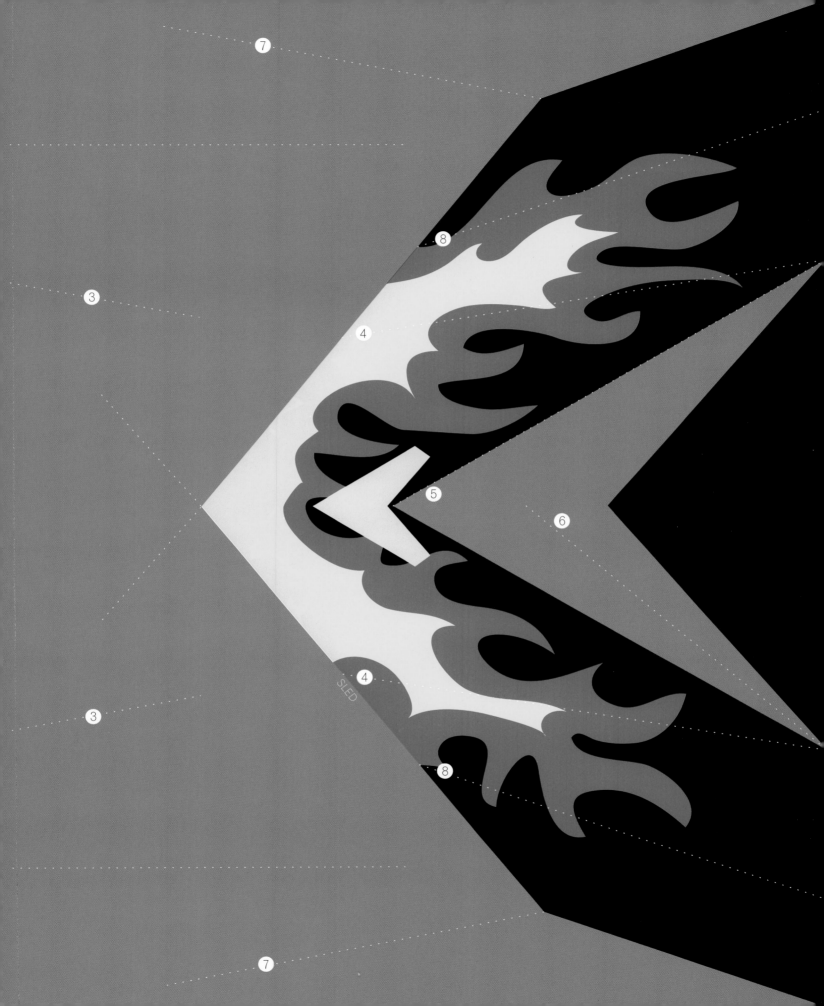

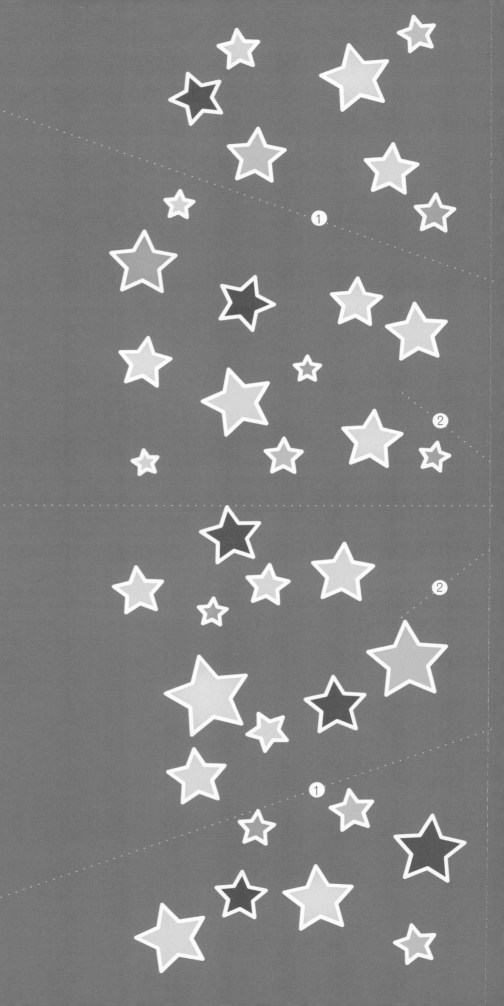

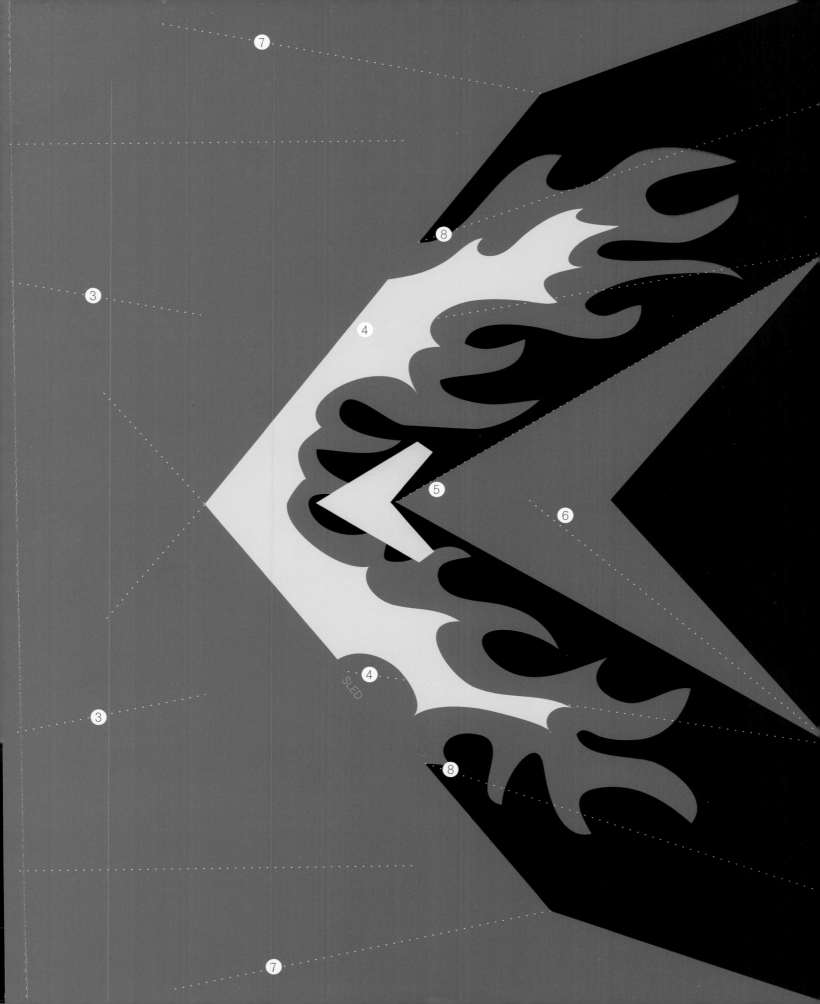